Library of
Davidson College

Library of
Davidson College

Legal Almanac Series No. 56

LEGAL RIGHTS IN THE ART AND COLLECTORS' WORLD

by SCOTT HODES

General Editor
Irving J. Sloan

1986
Oceana Publications, Inc.
Dobbs Ferry, New York

EDITOR'S NOTE

This book is an invitation to the artist and the collector to consider some of the legal ramifications involved in being an artist or being a collector. This discussion is designed for the layman, but it is not intended as a guide to being your own lawyer. Rather the book is intended to help the reader recognize when he has a legal problem and to communicate enough of the flavor of the law that he will be able to understand and work effectively with legal counsel. The author recognizes that the law, like art itself, may elude and confuse the uninitiated. If the flavor of the law has been lost or distorted in translation, the author must take full responsibility.

Library of Congress Cataloging-in-Publication Data

Hodes, Scott.
   Legal rights in the art and collectors' world.

   (Legal almanac series ; no. 56)
   Includes index.
   1. Law and art—Popular works.   2. Artists—
Legal status, laws, etc.—United States—Popular
works.   I. Sloan, Irving J.   II. Title.   III. Series.
KF4288.Z9H63   1985   344.73'097   85-28485
ISBN 0-379-11155-1   347.30497

© Copyright 1986 by Oceana Publications, Inc.

All rights reserved. No part of this publication may be reproduced or transmitted in any form or by any means, electronic or mechanical, including photocopy, recording, xerography, or any information storage and retrieval system, without permission in writing from the publisher.

Manufactured in the United States of America

TABLE OF CONTENTS

FOREWORD vii

Chapter 1
COMMERCIAL ART TRANSACTION 1

I. The Artist 1
   Commissions to Produce 1
   Death of Patron or Artist 5
   Sale through a Dealer 7
   Sale through Art Rental Outlets 10
   Mediation and Arbitration 11
   Code of Ethics 12
II. The Collector 12
   Auctions 15
   Legal Mechanics of an Auction 16
   Warranties at Auctions 18
   Specific Performance as a Remedy for
      Failure to Deliver 19
   Duty of Auctioneer to Seller 20
   Auctions and the Uniform Commercial Code 21
   Purchases from a Gallery or Private Person 22
   Rental Arrangements 23
   Purchasing from the Artist 24
   Syndications 26

Chapter 2
ART FORGERY—PROTECTION FOR
  ARTIST AND COLLECTORS 27

Chapter 3
LEGAL INVASIONS OF RIGHTS 35

   Invasion of Privacy 36
   Libel 38
   Disparagement 41
   Unfail Competition 42
   Imitation in Art 43
   Conclusion 44

Chapter 4
COPYRIGHT PROTECTIONS 45

- History of Copyright Legislation 45
- Federal Preemption of Copyright 47
- Copyright Term 48
- Improvement is Substantive Rights for
  Creators 51
- Copyright Formalities 53
- Deposit of Copies 55
- Copyright Registration 55
- International Copyright Conventions 56
- Conclusion 57

Chapter 5
TAX PLANNING AND THE ARTIST 61

- I. Income Taxes 61
  - Averaging Income—"Spreading Back" 61
  - "Spreading Forward" 61
  - Deduction of Expenses in General 62
  - Foreign Transactions 68
  - Prizes and Awards 69
  - Donating Art to Charity 70
  - Foreign Artists Earning Income in the
    United States 72
- II. Pre-Death Estate Planning 73
  - What Makes up the Artist's Estate and How
    it is Taxed 73
  - Computing the Tax 75
  - Valuation 75

Chapter 6
THE ART COLLECTOR AND TAXES 81

Chapter 7
INSURANCE MATTERS 89

- Insurance as Contract 89
- The Formation of an Insurance Contract 90
- Subject Matter of the Insurance Contract 91
- Types of Insurance Policies 92
- Art Work on Exhibition or Loan 94
- Loss or Destruction of Art Work 95

Chapter 8
INTERNATIONAL MOVEMENT OF ART 97

    Original Works 100
    Prints and Graphic Art 101
    Works of Art Produced by an American Artist
        Residing Temporarily Abroad 102
    Antiques 103
    Stained Glass Windows and Tapestrie 104
    Intended Use 104
    Export Restrictions 104
    General Customs Provisions 105
    Declaration for Customs 105

Epilogue 107

APPENDIX A
Glossary of Terms Reproduced from the Sotheby
    Parke Bernet Auction Catalogue 109

APPENDIX B
Artist-Dealer Contract/Artists Equity Assn. Inc. 119

APPENDIX C
Sample Forms for Planning Collectors' Estates 123

APPENDIX D
Art Appraisals 127

APPENDIX E
Agreement of Original Transfer of Work of Art 133

APPENDIX F
Model Consignment Agreement 137

APPENDIX G
Model Artist-Collector Agreement 141

INDEX 149

FOREWORD

This concise volume, growing out of years of work, is a most welcome and timely herald of awakening American interest in the fine arts. It must be a truism that any really serious human undertaking is soon codified and then relies on law to define its scope and defend its rights. As art bulks larger in the American consciousness, it progressively loses the frivolous mein imposed on it by our Puritan heritage and acquires dignity and honor that demands for it full and equal rights with other life-enhancing activity.

A review of the interrelations of art and the law over the centuries would show that commitments to produce art, to acquire art, to donate art, and to establish property rights in art often have led to legal action. The accounts of that action have contributed extensively to our knowledge of art history. Indeed, one may assume that most major works of art become a matter of public record through transactions of a legal nature that bring them into being. And while there are some hilarious pages in the record when artist and critic, or artist and patron, have clashed in court, and some humiliating passages when blundering officials attempted unsuccessfully to distinguish works of fine art from mundane materials, most of the record is solid and constructive. It provides a sound basis for resolving present and future problems.

One may take for granted that when millionaire dealers and patrons transact business in art their legal interests and problems are cared for adequately. One cannot safely assume as much for the artist, however, for his knowledge and resources ordinarily are meager. Too often he is the victim of his own special combination of ignorance of the law, generosity, and pride. This book is a shield for him.

The collector also needs guidance along the pitfall-paths of purchasing, importing, lending, and giving works of art, lest his innocent largesse reap troubles with tax collectors and customs officials. This book may be his salvation.

It is a mistake to think that anything about fine art is trivial. So great is popular esteem for art, if not for artists, that even worthless art is capable of exploitation. The painter or sculptor working at his trade may have no thought except for the sheer joy of creation, yet in effect he is creating his estate and its value to him and his heirs will depend upon how clearly he understands, or even senses, his rights and responsibilities. If he no more than senses them, in all probability he can find competent counsel, for I have noticed how the prestige and public status of art, together with its highly personal complications of taste and judgment, attract the best legal minds.

Although the author has confined himself in this book to the most general problems arising from sales, commissions, copyright, taxes, customs, and insurance, he has regularly summarized and interpreted the law to reveal its nature and intention. Accordingly, the imaginative reader will have no difficulty in seeing beyond usual horizons prescribed by habit and everyday experience. In a world of expanding media of communication, art remains the best all-around means of communication, therefore, it behooves the artist, and the collector of his work, to look over the horizon to future opportunities and hazards.

But, whatever the future may bring, the present holds problems enough in which this book can prove its usefulness. The traditional stereotype of the artist who is quite incompetent in business matters belongs to the present as well as to the past. How grateful this one is to the disreputable dealer who robs him; how angry and helpless that one who worked months on a portrait only to have it refused without payment; how stricken that other when costs of a commission ran higher than his fee! Too often the artist finds that he has traded his work for a puff of fame, yet even that satisfaction can be combined with tangible rewards if the artist knows his legal rights.

Nor is the art collector, although a businessman, likely to foresee in the specialized world of art all contingencies of acquiring, protecting, and conveying to others his artistic treasures. This book can aid him too. Here is one unhappily trying to satisfy the tax collector who thinks all of a painter's work must be of equal value regardless of date. There is another caught in the mills of customs and import regulations. This one learned too late of an advantageous way of giving his collection to the public. And that one paid for a forgery before seeking authentication.

To these beleaguered artists and collectors, and even more to their able associates whose common sense is often a reliable guide, this book is addressed. It is comprehensive and imaginative enough to contain some fresh facts, insights, or suggestions for everyone. Its great charm is that it discusses the law in layman's language, is not cluttered with references to cases, and frequently points out that some matters are so special in their circumstances and so complex in their ramifications that professional legal counsel should be sought. This is not a sue-them-yourself lawbook but is, instead, the lucid exposition by a good legal mind of common or typical problems created by conflicting interests in the field of art, together with possible remedies.

Possibly the greatest contribution the book can make is in the training of young artists in the art schools of America. I recall that not so long ago students, in their search for expression, were allowed to neglect basic technique until their disintegrating pictures literally became a scandal. Now the schools are teaching the fundamentals of sound technique. Yet, in my judgment it is far more scandalous to send young artists into the professional world with only the sketchiest knowledge of the ethics and business practices of art. I hope that our schools everywhere will require the study of the legal aspects of the artist's profession. A book such as this, therefore, is an essential resource.

Scott Hodes, the author and graduate of the University of Chicago, has had a personal interest in art since his undergraduate days and had an exceptional opportunity to live with and abet the growth of a private art collection. His efforts will be especially welcomed by all those artists who have been striving to give status to their profession through codes of ethics, standard contract forms, and similar instruments, some of which are reproduced in the Appendices. Equally, collectors will applaud and benefit from up-to-date information on government regulations as well as basic law affecting purchasing, customs, taxes, and insurance in the field of art. Indeed, anyone interested in the arts and their coming of age will find this valuable little book both fascinating and instructive.

The University of Chicago   Harold Haydon

Chapter 1
COMMERCIAL ART TRANSACTIONS
I. The Artist

I suppose that every serious artist expects to earn a decent living from his work. This is nothing to be ashamed of. An artist does not have to work in a drafty attic just to prove to the world that he is dedicated to his art. This does not mean, however, that an artist may not have to forego certain economic benefits while awaiting public acceptance. But every artist has a right, and even a duty to himself and his art, to attempt to sell his creations.

For better or for worse, selling a work of art projects the artist into the realm of business and law. A sale may be consummated in a variety of ways. The artist may choose to sell his work directly to a purchaser who intends to put the object in his own home; he may sell through a dealer or gallery; he may sell a finished work, or he may produce a work to meet certain specifications or tastes. But every arrangement presents different legal problems. The purpose of this chapter is to examine types of transactions artists are likely to enter and to warn against possible pitfalls.

Commissions to Produce

A commission is an agreement to purchase a work of art that does not yet exist but which the artist promises to bring into being. It is generally negotiated by the artist directly with his patron. The fact that the work does not exist when the agreement is reached causes most of the legal problems an artist is likely to encounter in accepting a commission. What if his patron is not satisfied and refuses to pay?

If the patron is not to be satisfied, his pronouncement

is not likely to come until the artist has almost completed his work. But what happens at this point will depend on the orginal agreement or contract. The die was cast long before.

Operationally, a contract may be defined as an agreement that will be enforced by a court of law. To be enforceable a contract must be founded on "consideration" (something of value to be given or done in exchange for something of value to be given or done by another). The law does not ordinarily force a person to keep a promise if he does not receive something in return. The theory is that there must be an exchange to support a contract. Illustratively, a promise to paint a picture for a person is not binding unless that person promises something of value (money or the like) in return. Generally, two acts are needed to create a contract. The first is an offer—"I will give you this, if you will give me that." The second is an acceptance—"Agreed."

An infinite variety of conditions or qualifications may be made a part of any contract. "This agreement is void in the event of a strike," or "if delivery is not made within thirty days," or "if I am not satisfied with the product," are terms frequently used. Satisfaction of the patron is a clause common to many artistic commissions, and it can be a very troublesome one for the artist.

The general policy of the law is to allow people to make any kind of contract they want, and to enforce that contract as written. This policy goes so far as to permit the making of contracts by which the duty of a party to perform his part of the bargain depends solely upon the state of his own mind—his own satisfaction. Therefore, if an artist enters a contract by the terms of which it is clear that the patron is to pay only if he is satisfied, the artist can collect only if he is able to achieve satisfaction on the part of his patron.

A person's state of mind is, of course, very hard to prove. Satisfaction is a state of mind. It is possible that a patron, having suffered a loss in the stock market, will decide that he wants to breach a contract and that he will feign dissatisfaction to avoid the appearance of a breach. It may be possible to convince a court that the disatisfaction is feined, but it will not be easy to do. If an artist makes this type of contract, he should be aware of the possible consequences.

Whether the artist finds himself completely at the mercy of his patron's whim may depend upon how the personal taste and satisfaction clause is written. If the contract says the artist shall be paid if he produces a "satisfactory" picture, the effect may be different than if the contract recites that the patron need pay only "if he is satisfied." Some courts may hold that a satisfactory picture is one that is objectively satisfactory; that is, one that would satisfy a reasonable man. In that event, proof of quality might be made by the expert testimony of other artists or of art dealers. However, most courts will interpret satisfaction clauses to require that the product satisfy the purchaser, unless it is completely unambiguous that the standard intended was the satisfaction of a reasonable man. The assumption is made, on the basis of general observations about human nature, that satisfaction of the purchaser is probably what was intended.

When working under a personal satisfaction contract, the artist should specify that his patron pay specified portions of the contract price at various stages of the creative process. Where this is not acceptable, the artist may gain some protection by having the patron put his initials on drafts, designs and preliminary sketches indicating that he is satisfied at various steps of the creative process. Then should the patron show reluctance to accept the final product, there is at least some evidence available from which it may be argued that the patron's dissatisfaction is not genuine.

If a dissatisfied patron cancels his contract, the artist will usually be entitled to dispose of the work elsewhere, unless it is a mural in the patron's house, of course. A portrait, however, presents a special problem. It may be an invasion of the patron's privacy, or even a form of libel if the subject is portrayed in a derogatory light, to sell or exhibit a portrait without authorization. If a portrait just cannot be completed to the patron's satisfaction, the artist may choose to hide or destroy his work, or he may swallow his pride and renegotiate the contract at a lower price. The only other possible choice is to obtain a written release from the subject permitting exhibition or sale.

If the reader will refer back to the sample "satisfaction" clauses discussed earlier, he will note that they were so phrased that they made the patron's duty to pay contingent on satisfaction. They did not promise satisfaction. If the artist says, "I will paint a satisfactory picture in return for so much money," he has promised to satisfy. Where that is true, a failure to satisfy will be a breach of contract by the artist, though geneally one with only minor consequences. Little damage has been done the patron except perhaps to waste some of his time. However, there may be fairly serious damage if the work of art is attached to the property of the patron. The patron may sustain costs in removing the unsatisfactory work, and to get what he wanted he may be requred to hire another artist at a higher price. In that case, damage may be assessable to the artist if he promised to satisfy. If the work of art will be affixed to the patron's property, it is especially important for the artist to use the contingent form, rather than the promissory form.

Where the work of art is a mural or becomes affixed in the house of the patron, the patron cannot retain the benefits of the artist's work, while at the same time refusing to pay. This is true even if the patron is not satisfied. There is a rule of law against unjust enrichment. In a situation of this nature, the artist is not entitled to receive his contract price because he did not fulfill his end of the bargain; however, he is entitled to a sum of money which adequately represents the value of his work. Theoretically, and as a practical matter too, the value of the artist's work should be less than the contract price since the original contract contemplated not only a work of a certain value, but one that corresponded exactly to what the patron wanted. That satisfaction should have some monetary equivalent over and above the value of the work on the open market.

Death of Patron or Artist

The contract between an artist and his patron is called a personal service contract. The patron is contracting for the services of a particular artist, and substitutes are not acceptable. This type of contract must be distinguished from one in which A contracts to give B's house a coat of paint. If A gets sick and cannot do the work himself, he may elect to find another painter to finish the job. B has no right to object because it makes little difference who does house painting so long as he is reasonably competent. But a man who hires Jackson Pollack is not likely to be satisfied if he gets a Norman Rockwell. And generally, the rights and duties under a personal service contract terminate with death or disability of either party, as would be expected.

In the absence of any language to the contrary in the contract, if performance by the promisor (artist) becomes impossible by virtue of death, insanity, or disabling illness, the contract is discharged, and the artist or his estate will be under no obligation. Likewise, if the work of art is a portrait, the patron or his estate will be under no obligation if the subject-either the patron or a third person-dies before there have been any sittings. If sittings are completed so that the artist can finish the painting without the subject, however, the patron or his estate would be liable for the agreed price. The result would probably be different if the artist had promised to "satisfy" the person who died. In this case, the contract would most likely be discharged for failure of consideration.

The rules discussed in this section are those that would be applied where the contract makes no provision for a contingency such as death, because that contingency was not contemplated when they entered the contract. Courts have rules, based on common sense, to help them guess what the parties to a contract would have wanted in a specific situation had they foreseen that such a situation might arise. Probably the main function of an attorney in the writing of a contract is to help his client to explore possibilities that would not ordinarily occur to the client, to advise the client to decide in advance how these possibilities should be dealt with, and to express the client's position in a manner that will be both clear and legally binding. When that is done, questions are less likely to arise in the first place. When they do, courts will not have to guess the intentions of the parties. Of course, the parties to a contract may decide to do exactly the opposite of what a court, shooting in the dark, would guess they would want done. As long as the result is not illegal or against public policy, the courts will go along. After all, one of the main doctrines of contract law is that the parties should be free to contract as they choose.

Sale through a Dealer

Probably the most popular method of selling art is to locate a dealer who will undertake to publicize and sell the artist's works. The dealer generally sells through gallery showings or exhibitions. In this way, art critics and the public are given an opportunity to see, evaluate, and purchase, the artist's works.

The artist and the art dealer may enter into one of two general arrangements, either of which may be varied in an infinite number of details. Basically, the dealer may purchase art and resell it, or serve as the artist's agent, selling on a commission or fee basis works that are owned, until sale, by the artist. As an example of variations within these two general classes, when the dealer buys he may agree to buy, and the artist promises to sell, the artist's entire output; the dealer may take a certain specified portion; he may have a right of first refusal; or he may just buy an occasional work. Where the dealer contracts to purchase all of the artist's output, the artist is bound by law to sell to the dealer every work he produces. Where the dealer has the right of first refusal only, and if the dealer decides not to purchase, the artist is free to sell to a third party.

If the paintings continue to belong to the artist while in the hands of the dealer, the dealer is an agent for the artist. In consideration of the dealer's services, the artist generally agrees that the dealer is to receive a commission or a fee. Such agency agreements may stipulate that the dealer is to have the exclusive right to sell the artist's works or that the artist is free to sell either on his own or through others. The agency relationship is subject to certain fixed legal rules, but an agency is set up by contract, so many of its terms may vary at the will of the parties.

In law, an agency has certain well-defined responsibilities. His fundamental role is to act on behalf of his principal, usually for certain limited and specified purposes. For example, an agent empowered to sell an artist's works would not also have the power to sell the artist's house. But the agency does have the power, as long as the agency relationship exists, to sell a painting or a sculpture, and the artist cannot interfere when the agent has contracted with a third party to sell one of the artist's works. The artist cannot come in and say, "I don't think you charged enough money for that piece," or "I've decided to keep that painting." In the absence of an agreement to the contrary, the agent (gallery) may bind the principal (artist) to any deal within the scope of the agent's authority.

An artist and a dealer may enter into an agency relationship by a formal, written contract, or by very informal means. For example, an artist may create an agency by leaving his work with the dealer, and it will be assumed that the artist consents to be bound by the contractual arrangements that are normally given by this dealer. Then, too, an agency to procure commission agreements for the artist may arise informally as the result of a stranger indicating that he knows a person who would like to commission the artist. If the artist accepts the commission, he will probably be bound to compensate the volunteer agent at a reasonable rate. Whether the artist leaves his work with the dealer or accepts a commission negotiated by a volunteer agent, the agency relationship, even though informal, may be a continuing one until definite steps are taken to terminate it. Basically, it is the artist as principal who is responsible for the creation of the agency relationship. Therefore, if the artist chooses to end the relationship, he must so advise the agent and also serve notice to the public, so that persons who may deal with the agent will not be misled.

The law also dictates that the dealer has certain recognized responsibilities toward the artist. The dealer must remain within the scope of the authority granted to him by the artist. If the artist has specified that certain pieces within the possession of the dealer are not for sale, the dealer must not violate this trust. The dealer cannot purposely sell the artist's work at a cut-rate price to his friends. Likewise, if the dealer fails to exert care for the artist's works that are in his possession, he may be held liable for their market value. Moreover, if the artist has given the dealer an exclusive agency agreement, the dealer must exercise reasonable efforts to publicize and sell the artist's work. Regardless of the type of contract that is negotiated between the artist and the dealer, the artist is not bound to perform unless and until the agent actually exerts some substantial effort on the artists' behalf.

Written contracts have certain advantages over informal agreements. By negotiating and commiting the terms of an agency relationship to writing, each of the parties will avoid many of the difficulties that may arise in the future. Obviously, it is better for the parties to have decided in advance how contingencies are to be handled, then to leave the question to judicial interpretation in a lawsuit. The failure to negotiate a binding contract at the inception of a working relationship has destroyed countless friendships and has consumed untold sums in legal fees and court costs. The contracts entered into between Henri Matisse and his dealer should be examined carefully, as they exhibit considerable ingenuity in solving problems that may well have arisen had Matisse merely left his paintings with a dealer and said, "Please sell them for me."

Sale through Art Rental Outlets

It has been estimated that there are approximately five hundred art collectors throughout the world who compose the market for high priced objects of art—those works priced at $50,000 or more. While the purchases and sales of these recognized individual art buyers make spectacular news, the art market does not exist on these transactions. As a matter of fact, the art market is not designed for these buyers. The average buyer is interested in works that sell for less than $300.

In an effort to penetrate the real art market and assist the up-and-coming artist, a museum or gallery will frequently offer an art rental service to its patrons. This service permits the artist to submit works of art in the hope that a collector will rent, and eventually purchase, his work.

Most contracts executed between an art rental agency and an artist stipulate that the artist shall set the selling price and that the rental agency is entitled to a specified commission or handling charge for its services. Frequently, too, the artist agrees to transport his works to and from the art rental outlet and assumes responsibility for any loss or damage that may occur in transit. Another provision may recite that the articles will not be cleaned or repaired either by the art rental service, or by the borrower, except with the written permission of the artist. Most rental services also agree to insure all items in their possession, with the understanding that potential liability will not exceed the selling price. As a measure to protect his copyright, the artist should insist that the agreement between the art rental outlet and the borrower specify that works of art will not be photographed, sketched, or otherwise reproduced without the express written consent of the artist.

Any agreement between the artist and rental agency should necessarily provide for termination of the relationship. This is generally effected by written notice from one party to the other. At the time of notification, the artist's works should be removed promptly from possession of the rental agency unless they are on loan at that time. In this event, the artist should wait until the article is returned by the borrower. Should the borrower exercise his option to purchase the work after the artist-agency agreement is terminated, but before the termination of the lease, the artist may not be entitled to the return of the article.

Over the past ten years, many art museums throughout the United States have opened art rental outlets. This vehicle has enabled the contemporary artist to expose the public to his works. It is of the utmost importance that the artist exercise great care when entering into a relationship with a rental agency. When doubtful about any provisions of their agreement, he is best advised to seek the assistance of a competent attorney.

Mediation and Arbitration

When an artist and his patron or an artist and his dealer develop a dispute, a third party may be asked to lend his good offices to help solve the problem. This is known as mediation and it in no way binds the respective parties. On the other hand, a dispute may be referred to a third party by mutual agreement of the parties, made either prior to the actual dispute in anticipation of foreseeable difficulty, or after the dispute has arisen. This type of an agreement, known as arbitration, will usually make the decision of the third party binding on the disputants.

When parties wish to have possible disputes settled by arbitration, they may use the services of the American

Arbitration Association. The Association maintains panels in more than thirteen hundred cities and, for a nominal fee, will supply a panel consisting of two or three Association members, frequently specialists in the field of dispute. The panel will generally conduct an informal hearing before handing down a decision.

Codes of Ethics

In an effort to bring order out of chaos in the field of art merchandising, codes of ethics have been adopted for the professional artist and for the commercial buyer of artwork by various Associations and Guilds. For the most part, these standards are predicated upon the belief that adherence to a code of fair practice will contribute to the welfare of the artist by establishing and building professional and public respect. The Code of Ethics of The Artists Equity Association is reproduced in Appendix J, and the Code of Fair Practice as formulated by the Joint Ethics Committee of the Society of Illustrators, the Art Directors Club and the Artists Guild is reproduced in Appendix I. These codes are modified from time to time by formal amendment or as a result of interpretation in hearings before the bodies that administer these codes.

II. The Collector

In purchasing a work of art, the collector pays for at least three different things—the quality of the work, the reputation of the artist, and the certainty that the named artist actually created the work. The prominent collector, Richard Rush, urges in his book *Art As An Investment* that the buyer look first for quality. That is sound advice; if the artist loses favor, as have many English landscape and portrait painters for instance, or if it is later proven that the painting had been wrongly attributed to a master when it was the work of a student, what is left but the painting? If it can be treasured for itself, the money spent for the work is not all lost.

If we limited ourselves to *nouveau riche* buying for investment, our audience would be limited indeed—not only because those people are relatively few in number, but because most have attorneys on retainer. The collector buyer modestly is probably investing his money in the safest manner. He may be purchasing the works of contemporaries or of the lesser lights of earlier times. In either event, he is likely to avoid one of the two pitfalls awaiting the unwary collector of expensive works—false attribution. And if the work purchased is pleasing, the modest buyer need not be seriously disturbed by market fluctuations. If prices fall, and they cannot fall too far, the opportunity to enjoy the work is likely to be worth the price. If they rise, the collector has a windfall.

It is the collector investing thousands of dollars in a single piece of art who must take extreme precautions to insure authenticity, for it is the big names whose works are forged or purposely copied. The collector who is ready to acquire the work of a great master must never forget the name of Hans van Meegeren, an obscure Dutch artist, who, during the days preceding the Second World War, forged and sold paintings that were accepted by well known critics as genuine Vermeers. The discovery that these were forgeries shocked the art world, for several had been purchased for hundreds of thousands of dollars by museums and prominent collectors. These works are now worth only a few hundred dollars, mainly as curiosities. From a legal point of view, it was debatable whether the crime of forgery had been committed by van Meegeren, since he did not imitate anything but only painted in Vermeer's style and manner. A list of van Meegeren's forgeries is included in Appendix A.

But forgery is by no means the only source of confusion respecting the attribution and authenticity of old paintings. Copying was once the standard method by which artists taught their apprentices, and to execute a good copy in the days before mechanical reproduction was considered thoroughly respectable. Today, in Europe there are literally painting factories turning out copies of paintings in the style of well-known artists. These copyists are not necessarily dishonest. But despite their best intentions, the attribution given a painting once it is out of their possession is also out of their control. The result is that there are doubtless tens of thousands of originally honest copies and probably thousands of intentional forgeries, created by more or less apt pupils, floating around to confuse the critic, the dealer, and the purchaser.

The collector can hardly be too careful in tracing the authenticity of a work. The first and preferred method is to make an effort to trace the ownership as far back as possible, even to the artist. Frequently, the back of a picture will have custom's stamps and other marks of pedigree, including who has owned it and where it has been exhibited. If this information is not available and the work seems worthy of further investigation because of apparent age and quality, a chemical analysis of the pigments can be made. Such an analysis can reveal the age of the pigments, and in some cases it is known whether a given pigment was available to or used by a given artist. Ultra-violet light can show whether a painting has been retouched. An expert can guess from the very brush strokes whether a work is genuine. This kind of research costs money; it is performed by the more important galleries, and it is for this reason that paintings cost more at such a gallery. The purchaser is paying for certain attribution these galleries can often provide.

The person who is knowledgeable in a certain school of

art and who buys for quality may well prefer to trust his own judgment on the value of a work. Such a person can save money at smaller galleries and auction houses where the facilities for authentication may be non-existent. But it is wise whenever a substantial sum of money is involved to have a work authenticated by one qualified to do so. A museum official or the art department of a local college may well be able to help. These institutions are often glad to do so, at least partly in the hope that someday the collector will donate works to them.

Auctions

One of the most common ways to buy and sell art is the public auction. This has long been true. Christie's auction house in London, still going strong, was in business at the time of the American Revolution. Today, the art auction is probably more popular than it has ever been. Since the end of the Second World War, prices for works of art, with some notable exceptions, have risen so rapidly that sales prices at larger auctions are often front page news.

The auction, at least theoretically, provides a means of accurately determining current market values. The "theoretically" must be added, because auctions are subject to manipulation and to waves of emotion. Bidding may be dampened by casting aspersions on authenticity or by art dealers who agree that only one of them will bid for a specific picture. If the one dealer is successful, the picture is then auctioned privately among the participating dealers, and they share the profit made at the second sale. If dealers have a surplus of works by a certain artist, they may bid up the price of a painting being sold at auction to give the impression that the particular artist is gaining in popularity. Waves of enthusiasm among collectors may also raise auction prices well above the level experts would consider reasonable. Still, as a general rule, auction prices are lower than those quoted at important galleries.

The owner of an art work may bid for his own property in the hopes of raising the price. This practice, where it is not made clear that the owner is bidding, is fraudulent. A purchaser may rescind a sale if it is later discovered that the owner or his agents were bidding to force up the price.

Legal Mechanics of an Auction

In law, an auction is simply a sale with a special method for determining price. There are special rules for auctions related to the bidding mechanism for setting price, otherwise, auctions are governed by the general laws concerning sales. Unlike statutory copyright legislation, which is national, the law of sales and auctions is local in character. Each state has its own sales and auction laws; there is, however, a general similarity among the states and many have adopted uniform acts drafted by panels of experts.

When an auctioneer puts a work of art up for sale, he is not making an offer to sell it to the highest bidder. It is the bidder who makes the offer. The auctioneer says in effect: "How much am I offered?" And, if he does not hear an offer he considers adequate, he may decline all those that are made. When a person responds with a bid that is recognized by the auctioneer, each prior bid is discharged. The last recognized bid is the only outstanding offer; the auctioneer indicates acceptance of the outstanding offer, or bid, by dropping his gavel. Any bidder (offeror) may, by giving notice to the auctioneer, withdraw his bid (offer) before the fall of the gavel. Once the gavel is banged, however, the bidder cannot change his mind. His offer has been accepted and a binding contract has been entered.

The auctioneer's corresponding right to withdraw a property from the sale exists unless the auction is described as "without reserve," or it is otherwise indicated that the goods will be sold to the highest bidder. The right to withdraw property from sale has been used to justify denying a person damages when, after traveling from Africa to New York to attend an auction, the auction was cancelled. The announcement of an auction, then, is no guarantee to a prospective bidder that an auction will take place. However, the terms of sale and other rules pertaining to the auction which have been advertised must be followed unless notice is given to the contrary.

Where a sale is without reserve, no lot may be withdrawn after even one bid has been made on it regardless of the auctioner's feeling that the bid price is too low. Lots may be withdrawn, however, before the bidding has begun. Consequently, the traveler, frustrated by having the auction cancelled, has no more protection when the auction is without reserve.

The reserve is usually a minimum price below which the auctioneer is not empowered to sell. Sometimes the reserve price may be advertised although, in practice, the upset price is generally kept secret. Auctioners prefer not to disclose the minimum price since too low a reserve may dampen the market. The reserve right may also be in the form of permission to the auctioneer to use his discretion in rejecting bids.

In the absence of special conditions of sale, title to the auctioned property passes when the gavel is knocked down and the auctioneer accepts the bid. With the passage of title to the buyer the risk of loss also passes. This means that the buyer bears any subsequent loss by fire or theft, unless otherwise specified by the terms of the auction.

Warranties at Auctions

The big auction houses, and undoubtedly reputable smaller ones as well, make no warranty of the catalogue description, authenticity, or condition of any paintings offered at auction. Their catalogues will usually set forth the terms and conditions of sale (see Appendix A). Purchasers are normally given the opportunity to examine the works before the auction so that they can determine whether the property is suitable for purchase. There is, however, a code commonly used in catalogue descriptions to indicate the gallery's position concerning attribution: The artist's full name indicates the greatest certainty; last name plus first initial lesser certainty; and the last name alone indicates a serious doubt of authenticity.

When an auctioneer does make a warranty, he or his employer is bound by it. If such warranties are given informally, they are nevertheless enforceable. This is especially true where the auctioneer is or purports to be knowledgeable and well-informed, and it is clear that the bidder is not an expert and is relying on the auctioneer's judgment. A catalogue description may also be taken as a warranty where there is no disclaimer. The fact that there have been very few cases in American courts concerning auction warranties on art or antiques suggests that art auctioneers are pretty careful about making claims.

The one thing the auctioneer or his principal clearly warrants is that he has good title to the picture he is selling. This means that no one can come to the buyer at a later date and claim that this piece is really his and the auctioneer had no business selling it. Where there is a defect in title and the auctioneer has revealed the name of the seller to the successful bidder prior to the auction, the purchaser's complaint should be directed to the actual seller. The point is that when the buyer knows the identity of the seller, he is, in effect, relying on the seller to deliver clear title. But where the true seller is not identified, the auctioneer is liable for any failure to pass good title. the auctioneer may also be liable to the buyer if other warranties have been given, although the legal test may be whether the warranty was made within the scope of authority given the auctioneer by the seller. This problem will not affect the right of the buyer to sue for damages or for rescission of the purchase; rather it will only determine who the buyer is able to sue. Where there is any doubt concerning the proper party sue, it is best for the buyer to join both the seller and the auctioneer as joint defendants.

Specific Performance as a Remedy for Failure to Deliver

The Anglo-American law has traditionaly been divided into two broad categories, law and equity. Equity developed in England in early modern times to provide remedies in situations where the traditional law courts were unable to assist. Law may have been unable to help because it gave no remedy at all, or because it gave an inadequate one. Basically, the only civil remedy at law was the payment of money. On the other hand, equity courts had the power to order people to do things other than to pay money. One equitable remedy is to order people to perform a contract, whereas a court of law could require only the payment of money damages when a contract was not performed.

Traditionally, courts of equity will not order the performance of a contract unless the subject matter of the contract is unique. Therefore, a plaintiff cannot seek an equitable remedy when a plaintiff who had agreed to paint his house refuses to do so. This plaintiff can only go to a court of law to ask for money damages, which is usually the difference between the price settled on in the contested contract and the price the plaintiff had to pay to find someone else to do the job. However, a plaintiff can file an action in equity to request specific performance when a gallery owner who agreed to sell a Rembrandt later changes his mind and refuses to deliver the painting. In this case, a court of equity will act because it is assumed that no money damages will be sufficient to purchase an equivalent to the Rembrandt painting, because there is no substitute for that particular painting. Most, if not all, contracts for the purchase of fine art works are specifically enforceable.

As a general matter there is no longer a distinction between a court of equity and a court of law. However, the traditional equitable remedies are still available only in those circumstances in which the old equity courts would act. The remedy of specific performance, a traditional equitable remedy, would be available in appropriate circumstances regardless of whether the purchase was made at an auction, a gallery, or from a private individual.

Duty of Auctioneer to Seller

The occasion may arise when a collector decides to dispose of some or all of his works by means of an auction. The auctioneer is the owner's agent, subject to the same general rules of the agency as is the gallery that sells an artist's works on a commission basis. There is no problem, however, respecting giving public notice that the agency-relationship of an auctioneer is terminated. It is generally recognized that such an agency terminates with the conclusion of the auction.

The auctioneer has the same duty to the owner as the gallery to the artist—to care for the works put in his possession. Both are, as holders of the works, bailees for hire. The bailee for hire (a person paid to hold or handle the goods of another) is bound to exercise what is called ordinary care—the care a person would take of his own property. This rule applies where there is no specific contract detailing the degree of liability assumed by the bailee. A gallery or auction house will prefer, of course, to reduce its own liability as bailee, either by contracting out or by making arrangements for insurance. In dealing with a bailee, an artist or owner should want to clarify the degree of the bailee's liability and is strongly urged to arrange for either himself or the bailee to purchase adequate insurance coverage.

Auctions and the Uniform Commercial Code

The Uniform Commercial Code, like other uniform state laws, is the product of a commission of experts who draft laws in various fields and urge their adoption by all states. The Uniform Commercial Code has been adopted in a number of states. The Code covers sales, including auctions, negotiable instruments, and other commercial transactions. The sales section is an outgrowth of an earlier Uniform Sales Act, also adopted in a number of states. Uniform laws among the states on commercial matters are of considerable assistance in simplifying interstate commerce.

In most of the states in this country, the laws of contract and commerce are based on the common law of England. Yet, over the years the judges in various states differed in their interpretation of the common law. The uniform acts were designed both to simplify interstate dealings through uniformity and to select from among the decisions of the various states those rulings on specific questions that seemed most desirable. The mechanics of an auction described on pages 16 and 17 are those provided by the Uniform Commercial Code. Essentially the same approach is followed in states that have not adopted the Code. The same comments could be made respecting the relation of uniform laws of sale and the common law of sales in the various states.

Purchase from a Gallery or Private Person

In an auction, price is set by bidding; the terms of sale and applicable warranties are usually settled by the rules for the auction circulated by the auctioneer. In a direct sale, price, warranties and terms of purchase are proper subjects of negotiation, though some galleries may set their terms and leave it to the purchaser simply to accept or reject them. No rules can be given for effective bargaining, other than that the purchaser should keep in mind that he has at least three matters to settle when he does make a direct purchase.

As suggested earlier, price may be contingent on certain other aspects of the deal. For example, a preferential price may be given for cash. Then, too, the price is likely to be higher when dealing with experts willing and able to authenticate a work.

In the majority of cases, well-known galleries have sufficient knowledge or sufficient concern with their reputation to be willing to guarantee a work; where that is not true, at least a guaranteed history of ownership may be available. And some galleries, in lieu of, or in addition to other guarantees will enter into buy-back agreements. Buy-back contracts can be written so as to require the gallery to repay the purchase price or to credit the purchase price or value toward another work whenever the purchaser should want to return the picture. They may also limit the responsibility to buy-back to certain situations, such as when doubt is cast upon authenticity. The terms of the buy-back agreement are also subject to negotiation. In dealing with the established gallery, one is reasonably certain to find one or another of these procedures adopted as a standard method of operation. As long as the adopted method provides reasonable protection there is probably little point in bargaining for a variation.

Lesser galleries usually sell art more cheaply; they are more interested in rapid turnover and they usually lack facilities for authenticating. They are less likely to be willing to guarantee authenticity. Many reasonable and sometimes very excellent buys may be found in such galleries, but the buyer must be willing to rely upon his own taste and artistic erudition in making a selection.

Despite the fact that the reputable lesser gallery may be reluctant or unable to give guarantees on the authenticity of any but contemporary works, warranties may, in some instances, arise more or less unintentionally. In states that have adopted the Uniform Commercial Code, any factual description or assertion, verbal or written, is likely to gain the status of a warranty. Statements of opinion or value, however, usually do not give rise to warranties, though they may where the buyer reasonably relies upon the opinions expressed by the seller. There is reasonable reliance where an amateur or lay person relys upon opinions expressed by a person who holds himself out as an expert.

Warranties that might otherwise come into being respecting possible defects or conditions that could be detected by a surface examination are waived when the purchaser examines the item or refuses to do so despite a specific request of the seller. Warranties against hidden defects are not waived by the buyer's examination. The reasons behind these rules should be obvious.

Rental Arrangements

Two types of rental arrangements are widely used. The first is a straight rental agreement where the borrower is expected to return the piece at the end of the rental period. The second is a rental-purchase plan, whereby the rental fee may be applied to the purchase price. The first type is used by institutions with premanent circulating collections; the second is used primarily by galleries or rentals outlets in museums whose main concern is selling to the public.

The rental purchase plan is particularly attractive to buyers who are looking for works of art that they can enjoy. This plan permits the borrower to live with an object for a period of time before making a final commitment to purchase. This arrangement serves much the same function as the buy-back but is probably more advantageous for the gallery or rental outlet that accepts works of art on consignment.

The rental agreement itself is usually a very simple document. The borrower agrees to use the picture for display in his own home only, to respect the common law copyright, and to be liable for damage or deterioration resulting from his gross negligence. Insurance against other risks will usually be provided. The borrower should make sure, however, that he understands just what protection is specified in the agreement. (See Appendix B for sample of rental agreement.)

The rental-purchase plan provides, in addition, that the rent paid may be applied toward the purchase price. A two month period seems to be a commonly accepted rental period, although one or more renewals may be permitted. A Chicago gallery, for instance, using the rental-purchase plan allows a two month rental and a two month renewal, the rent for both periods being applicable to the purchase price.

Purchasing from the Artist

With the spread of art fairs, another phenomenon of

the post-war art boom, more and more individuals have easy and direct access to practicing artists interested in selling their works. Artists displaying at fairs range from rank amateurs to those having achieved substantial local recognition. The well-established artist, however, is less likely to exhibit for several reasons. First, he may have an exclusive sales arrangement with a gallery; second, he may be executing more ambitious works for which he would have to charge more than the typical art fair patron is prepared to spend; or third, he may simply find an art fair more exhausting and time consuming than it is worth. The mere fact that a recognized artist is less likely to display his work at an art fair should not discourage a collector from buying at a fair. In fact, works of good quality can often be obtained quite reasonably, and there is no middle man or dealer to be compensated. There is, of course, no problem with attribution; the only question is the quality and price of the work. Since a sale is often consummated on the spot, there is a little likelihood that problems pertaining to delivery of the piece will arise unless an arrangement is made to pay for and pick up a work at a later time. About the only type of warranty that might be inferred in this type of a transaction is that the work is done in such manner that it will not immediately fade or disintegrate.

What is true for a purchase at an art fair is true for any direct purchase from an artist. Complications are likely to arise only where works are commissioned or where the artist has an exclusive sales arrangement with a dealer or gallery. If the latter situation arises, a person who purchases from the artist without knowledge of the agency relationship will have no responsibility to reimburse the agent for a commission. It is the artist who will have breached his contract and most probably be subject to a lawsuit for damages. On the other hand, if the purchaser is aware of the artist's contract with a dealer, the purchaser may be subjected to a claim for commissions by the dealer. The prudent buyer should inquire if the artist has such a relationship, but it is not clear just how exhaustive this inquiry must be to claim that a purchase was consummated without knowledge.

Syndications

With the prices of great masterpieces rising to phenomenal levels, it is not uncommon for groups of art dealers or private investors to purchase these art objects, either for immediate resale or to hold as a long term speculation. Generally, these groups form a syndicate or partnership and each member holds an undivided interest in the property proportional to his respective investment. It may be assumed that persons who enter such agreements are sophisticated art investors and do so with appropriate legal advice.

In a syndicate purchase, the participant is generally approached by a promoter to invest a certain sum of money in return for an undivided interest in the work of art. Where the promotor approaches a great number of prospective investors, there may be some question as to whether the undivided interest is a "security" subject to the provisions of the Securities Act of 1933 as amended. The chief purpose of this Act is to obtain full, fair, and accurate disclosure of the character of securities offered for sale in interstate commerce or through the mails and to prevent fraud in the sale of securities. If a person is contacted by an art syndicate promoter, he is best advised to check out the deal thoroughly and to consult an attorney before committing himself.

Chapter 2
ART FORGERY — PROTECTION FOR ARTISTS AND COLLECTORS

There have been many hoaxes and forgeries through history; Van Meergen's faked Vermeers are among the most notable. In many of these situations, as with Van Meergen's forgeries, the works of art were enjoyed and mistaken for the originals. They provided aesthetic pleasure for the average person, and even the experts could not tell the difference. Why then do we brand such works as forgeries or fakes and provide legal penalties and remedies? In what context are these remedies and penalties established, and how adequate are they? Why do we have such difficulty in accepting a work of art once we have discovered it as a forgery? The "fake" painting or other work of art has the aesthetic qualities of composition, color, harmony, power, and whatever else one wants to attribute to the aestheticism. Logically, there is no reason not to accept the work and value it.

Other cultures like the ancient Egyptians and Chinese made no distinction between copies and originals. There was no stigma attached to acquiring or making a copy. The Romans and Greeks commissioned and collected copies. During the Renaissance an acknowledged imitation could bring as much as half the price of the original. In the seventeenth century Emperor Rudolf II sent court painters to copy the best of Venice and Rome. Experts today still have trouble distinguishing these paintings from the originals. In Germany, if a work in one of their museums was determined to be a fake, the work *nach* ("in the manner of") was put before the artist's name. The work could then be celebrated for its own merits and appeal. The art historian, Walter Pach wrote: "Until modern times copies, imitations, and even forgeries were made by men of such talent that the works possess qualities connoisseurs value in themselves." Today, however, our experience and view of art has shifted along with changes in culture, economics, and aesthetic values.

In recent years the exigencies of the art market and its development into a free trading international market have given ingenious forgers and ordinary confidence men plenty of opportunity for swindling the art buying public. There has been an increase of public awareness of art and an increase in the number of people who can afford to buy these works. They have proven to be, in many cases, a more attractive investment than the stock market. In these inflationary times when people tend to turn to collectibles to preserve the value of their money, art works have been a favorable investment. They have reacted to the market forces of supply and demand, increasing tremendously in value as the supply of authentic works remain relatively constant while consumer demand rises.

The market forces and structure of art have set the stage. The art forger steals the scene by taking advantage of the situation. Since the advent of art forgery as a recognizable offense, authorities and victims have sought to eradicate it because the risk of conviction for sale of an art forgery is relatively small. There are several reasons for this. On one side stands the scientist with his technical equipment for detection of fraud. However, he must rely upon the art experts. It is the historian's or connoisseur's trained eye that first detects the possibility of the forgery, thus alerting the technicians. These experts are not available to everyone desiring to buy art and there are no licensing agencies, ethical committees, or competency exams to control the quality and validity of these authentications. The situation is ripe for negligent or incompetent advice. On the other side stands the forger who has all the modern technical and artistic resources available to aid in his attempt to stay one step ahead of the authenticators. In the middle are the galleries, the collectors, and the directors of museums. These participants many times unwittingly aid the forger. They often are hesitant in the face of costly advice, huge publicity, and a desire not to besmirch the good name of the art market or their own good names to admit publicly they have bought a forgery and thus fail to cooperate in criminal prosecution. If a fraud is reported the victim dealers are afraid they will lose customers, and the victim collectors are afraid they will lose the value of their bargain if the fraud becomes known. So they both remain silent—one to preserve his supposed integrity and one to preserve the supposed "authenticity" of his purchase.

The sympathies of the general public often tend to side with the forger. We see something glamorous in somebody with the skill and cunning to produce a work the apparent equal of a great master. We somehow do not see this crime as being aggressive or as debilitating as others. In short, the crime of the forger is not violent, it is just cunning.

Taking all the foregoing factors into account and considering: (1) there are jurisdictional problems due to the international nature of the art market, and (2) that presently both federal and state laws are inadequate in specifically dealing with this problem, the risk of conviction for the sale of forged art remains relatively small. Although all states have penal statutes that prohibit forgery, these statutes do not deal specifically with the marketing of fake paintings or art forgery as a distinct statutory crime. Prosecutions generally fall under laws dealing with conspiracy, larceny, and fraud which are not conducive to effective art forgery deterrence.

A work of art has been defined as an aesthetic

expression that is a product of a particular time, place, and person. A fake pretends to this but is not. If a person wants to buy a fake and pays a proper price there is no legal problem. "The essential feature of art forgery is not imitation, which may have many other motives, but the intention to deceive either the general public or an individual dupe or as a rule; prospective buyers." (2 J. Merryman & A. Elsen, *Law and the Visual Arts* 6-87) Therefore, to obtain a conviction the essential element is fraudulent intent. To obtain the necessary proof of intent in a criminal prosecution for art forgery under these statutes and to carry the burden of proof beyond a reasonable doubt is difficult. It is easy for the faker to claim he had no knowledge the fakes would be sold as originals. It is easy for the dealer to claim he thought the works were authentic.

It is also sometimes difficult for the prosecution to prove beyond a reasonable doubt the painting is indeed a fake. Scientific analysis is not foolproof and the appraisals of experts are just expressions of opinions which juries and judges may not find convincing. The prosecution must prove a connection between the fake and the faker which is costly and many times more difficult because the chain of title or origins of the work often can be difficult to trace. This is further complicated by the international nature of the art market.

The Uniform Commercial Code can be an effective remedy in many forgery situations. The warranty provisions (sections 2-313, 2-314, 2-315, 2-316) if used effectively and creatively can provide relief to the unwary and duped victims of art forgery. Nevertheless, the Code has failed more than it has succeeded when invoked in these kinds of cases.

New York has led the way in terms of art related legislation. This seems to be a logical outgrowth of New

York's status as a leading art market and the continuing problems of preventing art forgery and providing sufficient remedies. Illinois and California have attempted to follow New York's lead. Such legislation can significantly affect the art market by setting standards of behavior or customs of the trade. In regard to forgeries, sales of works of art not warranted under New York law will not be readily accepted in other markets. Disclosures relied upon by buyers under New York law will most likely not be ignored in other markets not subject to the same markets.

Under section 170.45 of the Penal Law, New York has made art forgery a separate punishable offense. It makes "fraudulent misrepresentation and simulation of antiques, *objects d'art,* rare books and comparable matter" a misdemeanor. However proof of criminal intent is still necessary and it is questionable whether a penalty of up to a year in jail is sufficient deterence given the huge profits to be made through forgeries. (See Appendix C.)

Articles 12-C of the New York General Business Law attempts to protect the artist by imposing a trust obligation on the dealer. (See Appendix D.)

Article 12-H of the New York General Business Law, better known as New York's visual multiples disclosure bill, is a relatively new section regarding works of art. This legislation was passed as a result of New York's dominant position as a center in the art market and its continuing effort to legislate in the art field to prevent art fraud. The corrupting of this market, and disillusionment on the part of the collector could cause the bottom to fall out of the market.

The worst offenses with regard to art forgery arise in the field of prints. Lithographs are especialy vulnerable as today's technology makes it easy to fool the public into thinking photo-mechanical lithographic reproductions are real lithographs. In the past twenty years abuses have increased tremendously as the market has grown. Previously, prints did not bring enough money to make forging them worthwhile. However, this small market has grown to do an estimated business of $125 million to $150 million a year for modern prints along. An increase in demand has caused prices to increase tremendously. People can now own original works by well-known artists by purchasing limited edition fine prints at a fraction of the cost of a drawing or painting by the same artist. Due to the multiplicity of the print, a collector can ascertain its value at a particular time through auction results or prices asked by other dealers for the same print. This certainty creates a greater feeling of security for the buyer and enhances the desirability of prints as an investment.

The basic problem with a print occurs when trying to distinguish between an "original" print and a reproduction. The aesthetic value is controlled by the degree of active participation of the artist and is diluted to the extent that the work is done by others. There is a difference in the artistry involved between an "original" print and a reproduction, thus, there exists a disparity in value.

This new law in New York, which covers prints and photographs sold for $100 and up, is an attempt to design a law that would deter deceptive print practices, thwart misleading advertising and provide purchasers with the information for making an intelligent choice by legally requiring the disclosure of certain facts that, as the law points out, most reputable dealers already furnish voluntarily. It protects the buyer's right to full disclosure. It is an attempt by the legislature to stifle such practices as the use of editions "stretched" by an undisclosed and unusually large number of artist's proofs, undeclared closely related editions, misrepresented reproductions and claims that a work is "signed" by the artist when the signature is that of another. The law never uses the terms "original" or "fine print." The criterion is whether it is the artist's print approved by the artist after completion. (See Appendix E.)

To accomplish its purpose article 12-H is divided into sections according to the availability of information. Prints dated from 1950 to 1981, 1900 to 1950, and prior to 1900 require progressively less requirements of disclosure as the availability of information diminishes due to the age of the print. Only information which is reasonably obtainable is required. The dealer must provide certain basic information in writing which is considered part of the basis of the bargain creating an express warranty. This warranty cannot be negated by the merchant for lack of the use of formal words of warranty, or for the lack of intention or authorization to make a warranty, or because the statement could be interpreted as the seller's opinion. If the information provided is erroneous, the buyer is entitled to a full refund. If the buyer can prove that the seller willfully failed to provide the required information or knowingly provided false information, the buyer may be able to collect treble damages and attorney's fees from the seller. Such information as the actual total number in the edition including the artist's proofs must be revealed if the print is represented as being from a limited edition. Also, a statement as to the authenticity of the artist's signature, the year executed, the medium used, and whether the work was authorized by the artist if there is no signature must be provided.

The impact of this law is significant in that it provides an enforcement mechanism through its penalties previously lacking in similar versions adopted in California, Illinois, Maryland, and Hawaii.

Some objections to the law have been raised by dealers who claim that the information necessary to complete a transaction provides undue paper work and expense, complicating the process. Some artists complain that requiring disclosure of the total number in a limited numbered edition is too restrictive as they cannot wait to see how an edition will be received and how it sells. If an artist miscalculates and issues too many, the value inherent in scarcity is lost. However, these objections have been overcome when weighed against the potential contribution of this article to the stability and integrity of the market, and its important benefits provided to the collector who would otherwise have little recourse. Article 12-H helps establish a basis for values. The fair market value of these prints is based partly on scarcity. It is pertinent for the collector in determining estate taxes, and it is necessary for the seller who warrants his product and must make refunds or absorb penalties if labeling is inaccurate.

Earlier proposals of this law had included sculpture which is a runner-up to prints in the fraud market. But it was not included due to an intention of giving it separate consideration in another law that deals specifically with sculpture. The problems with regard to sculpture are similar to those of prints. Significant is the number of casts which have been made. Multiplicity of casts creates the potential for forgery, unauthorized editions, excess production, and inferior reproduction which might be dealt with through specific legislation within the next few years.

Chapter 3
LEGAL INVASIONS OF RIGHTS

Art is a mode of visual perception and reflects the way the artist sees the world about him. The naive person insist that there is only one way to see the world—the way that it appears in his own immediate vision. This is not true, since we see what we learn to see, and our vision becomes by habit a careful selection of all that there is to see. What we want to see is determined by our desire to discover or construct a meaningful world. Art in that way becomes a construction of the artist's reality.

In constructing his version of reality, the artist must be concerned with a series of legal wrongs that he may commit in the creative process, or that may be perpetrated upon him in the practice of his profession. The law which permeates the artist's environment, serves to protect an individual from suffering either personal or economic injury. Protection is accorded by permitting recourse to the courts in the following circumstances: (1) where the details of a person's life, his name, his reputation, or a pictorial representation of him are appropriated without obtaining proper consent, there is an *invasion of privacy;* (2) where the property of an individual is unlawfully appropriated for economic gain, it is *unfair competition;* (3) where an untrue statement damages a person's reputation or standing in the community, it is *libel* (written statement) or *slander* (verbal statement); and (4) where an untrue statement damages a product or property, it is *disparagement*. At times, it is difficult to distinguish between wrongs. "John Doe makes a lousy violin," might be interpreted as libel against John Doe, disparagement of his violin, or both. These wrongs and their legal consequences are the subject matter of this chapter.

Invasion of Privacy

The concept that it is a tort, or personal injury, to expose the name, picture or details of the life of a private citizen is based on the belief that there is an innate right to be left alone — a so-called right of privacy. Invasion of privacy, as an actionable common law tort, came into being in the late 1890's on the theory that, in an increasingly complex society, with a press demanding more and more material for publication, it was necessary to protect a person's right simply to be left alone. Because of its relatively recent development, the law respecting the right of privacy has not developed to the same extent as the law respecting long established torts. Consequently, there is confusion about even quite fundamental issues in this field of the law.

Generally, a person who is not newsworthy has the most compelling argument in favor of protecting a right of privacy. However, even those who have become newsworthy may object to an unsolicited invasion of their private lives when exposure is unrelated to their public image or activities. While it is appropriate to discuss or comment on those aspects of a politician's life that affect his suitability for public office, the details of his family life are generally private, unless he chooses to make them public (as politicians with large and attractive families do). A person, then, may voluntarily place in the public domain aspects of his life that could not otherwise properly be the subject of comment and criticism.

There are circumstances, however, where the private life of a person is sufficiently interesting to the public that publication without actual or implied consent is permissible. Of course, this statement assumes that the publication is not defamatory or too intimate. A leading case in this area concerned *The New Yorker* magazine profile of a child prodigy who had in his mature years retreated into obscurity. The fact that this person had once been newsworthy and that the public had a reasonable interest in what had happened to him were considered adequate justifications for publishing a report of his present day circumstance.

The artist is most likely to commit the tort of invasion of privacy by producing and showing a representation of a person without permission. The point has already been made that an artist whose portrait of a subject were rejected might commit an invasion of privay by showing it or disposing of it to a third person. Obviously, the details of a person's private life may be exposed graphically, rather than in words. Obviously, too, a visual work depicting someone who is well known may have increased value. If produced without permission of the subject, such a work may fall in that hazy area where invasion of privacy and unfair competition meet. One way for the artist to guard against a lawsuit for an invasion of privacy is to ask for written releases from all parties concerned. Care should be exercised when a minor is involved, since releases from minors are void and must be executed by the parent or the guardian. The release should include the purpose to which the released material is to be put. A model release is reproduced in Appendix F.

The artist may, of course, be subjected to invasions of his own privacy. He has a right to protect himself from reports of his personal life (though not from comments on his work). Moreover, the artist may resort to a court of law to enjoin others from profiting from the use of his name or his likeness.

The vast majority of cases involving an invasion of privacy occur where there has been a fairly wide publication or distribution of the material constituting the invasion. Mere word-of-mouth comments (unless uttered on radio or television) probably will not support an action for invasion of privacy, although this issue is still largely unresolved. On the other hand, the amount of publication necessary to support a case for libel or slander has been more thoroughly litigated over the years, and in those cases the most minimal publication will generally support a case.

Libel

Any defamatory material which tend to degrade a man in the eyes of his neighbor or to injure his property or business may be considered libelous and give rise to a cause of action for damages suffered. Since libelous material may be published by a writing, an effigy, or a picture, it is therefore advisable for the artist to consider carefully the subject matter of his work before it is published or exhibited.

In most states, no specific injury to the plaintiff needs to be shown in order to collect damages; the injury is presumed from the publication and the character of the statement. The actual damage in a libel case is not harm to the feelings of the person libeled, but the effect on his reputation in society. A person has a right to protect the public image he wishes to display, and it is no defense to a libel charge to argue that most people would not consider the statement defamatory. In a sense, then, libel is the very opposite of invasion of privacy. In an invasion of privacy, the right protected is to have people unaware of one's life—it might be called the right to withdraw, whereas the right to be free from libel is a protection of one's public image.

At times, it is difficult to determine whether certain material will be held libelous. Statements or graphic portrayals may not outwardly appear to libel anyone, or they may accidently libel a person with whom they are not actually concerned. In the first category are statements that do not make direct reference to a specific person but refer to and identify that person by a set of circumstances that would be familiar to some people. In the second category are cases of unintended reference—where, for example, one man is described and something is said of him which, if untrue, would be libelous, and then another man appears who fits this description or who carries the same name. An example of an unintended reference occurred when a newspaper printed a photograph of a man and woman with a caption indicating an intended marriage. In fact, this man was already married. His wife promptly sued the newspaper and received a judgment on grounds that friends and acquaintances inferred that she was not the wife but, instead, the mistress of the man pictured in the newspaper. In this case, the libellant (newspaper) did not even refer to the plaintiff—the wife—and the statement itself was not libelous but only damaging when taken in conjunction with the fact, of which the libellant had no knowledge, that the man was already married. In a few states, it is required that where a libel is not clear and complete in itself, the plaintiff has the burden of proving special injury in order to receive a judgment. In these states the inference that there must have been injury is abandoned.

A libel must also be published, which means simply that it must be read by some third party. Therefore, it is not libelous to send an insulting letter to a person, but if the letter is sent by messenger in an unsealed envelope and he reads it, or if it is sent by post card so that post office employees can read it, libel may be found. However, if the recipient permits a private, defamatory letter to be read, the sender is not guilty of publishing. On the other hand, where the sender knows the recipient to be blind or illiterate so that the letter will have to be read to him, the sender is guilty of publishing a libel.

In a charge of libel, the defendant may respond with the defense that the publication was truthful. However, the burden of proving the truth of the statement is on the defendant. The defendant cannot merely say that he believed the statement true, or that it was told him on good authority, or that the plaintiff had the reputation of doing what was reported. The defendant must actually prove that his statement is essentially true, although some variance in detail is permitted. By placing the burden of proving truthfulness upon the defendant, libel suits become rather difficult to defend. And where the libel charged alleges the comission of a crime, the defendant asserting the truth of his statement may even have to prove it beyond a reasonable doubt—that is, according to the standard of proof that would be used in a criminal court, rather than the civil standard, which is preponderance of the evidence.

Besides asserting that a statement alleged to be libelous is true, a defendant in a libel suit may raise other affirmative defenses. If the plaintiff consents to the libel by publishing the statement himself, or the communication is privileged, the defendant may properly defend his case. Privileged communications include the transmittal of information, damaging or not, where the recipient, an employer or lender for instance, has a legitimate interest in knowing the type of information communicated, or where the sender is attempting to protect his interests or those of one near to him. In the public sphere, one may repeat a statement found in public records and not be guilty of libel, though the statement be false. There will be, of course, a differnce of opinion of how public a record must be to qualify in support of this defense.

Another defense to a lawsuit for libel is the right to offer fair comment. For the artist, fair comment is a two-edged sword. The artist may justly comment on, or even ridicule in words or in graphic art, the works of others. He is, of course, subject to the same sort of comment and criticism from others. Every man who publishes, commits himself to the judgment of the public.

It should be evident throughout this discussion that there is no requirement of intent before finding a person guilty of libel. One can libel quite accidentally. Whether a libel is innocent or malicious will be taken into consideration in assessing damages but not in determining whether a libel has been committed.

Disparagement

Disparagement is a form of defamation that reduces or even destroys the value or marketability of property. As in a case of libel, disparagement must be published to a third party, it must be untruthful, and it must refer to the plaintiff. It may, however, be written or spoken and, unlike a libel action, injury is not presumed but must be proven. Just because the artist is unable to sell his work as a result of a disparaging remark, the person who uttered the statement is not necessarily at fault and liability must be demonstrated.

It has been held that a statement charging that a gallery represented a copy to be the original was disparaging where the picture was the original. It has also been held, surprisingly enough, that a publisher had an action for disparagement when it was said of one of its textbooks that it was a laughingstock among intelligent teachers. I use the word "surprisingly" for it would seem that this statement would come within the range of fair comment on literary and artistic matters. And even where it is shown that the artist or author has been unable to sell his products as a result of a disparaging remark that would be called a fair comment, the person who uttered the remark is not liable.

It is also not defamatory to "puff" one's own products, even where there is an implied criticism of another's. A man may generally say, "I produce the best baby-food" or that "oil is safer than gas for heating." If the artist makes a statement to the effect that his work is superior to that of another artist, it may be protected under the recognized privilege to "puff" and also as a fair comment on the work of another. In criticizing the work of another the artist must recognize that there is a fine distinction between fair comment and disparagement.

Unfair Competition

Where an artist's work has gained a certain value, it is a form of unfair competition for another party to reap that value without consent. This legal theory was discussed in the chapter on copyrights, but it is worth repeating that this tort encompasses the wrongful appropriation of an intangible.

Under certain circumstances the prohibition on unfair competition will protect the title of a work of art even though a title is not subject to copyright. This is especially true where a novel has been very successful and a movie producer uses the title to cash in on the reputation of the novel. The title of a painter's work, however, may be subject to wrongful appropriation and exploitation if it is as famous as the "Mona Lisa" or "A Sunday Afternoon on the Island of La Grande Jatte."

In many respects, the law of unfair competition resembles the law against invasion of privacy. The latter guards against the appropriation of intangibles that are intentionally kept out of the market place. The former protects against the appropriation of those intangibles that are intended to be commercially exploited. In either case, something of value has been taken from the creator.

Imitation in Art

Lawsuits for plagiarism are more prevalent in works of fiction, drama and music, than in the graphic arts. undoubtedly, this paucity of litigation over purported imitation in the graphic arts is a direct result of the artist's understanding that a given period will produce many works of art similar in style and theme. Mature artists understand that art is a combination of personal physical and mental experiences which are often influenced by the style of other matters. The work of such masters carries an impact that results in waves of influence on younger or less experienced artists. These recognized artists need not necessarily be indignant when they find many of their ideas are used by other artists. Sometimes this is a source of gratification.

In any event, a reticence to press litigation for plagiarism is probably a good thing. It is not desirable that the intellectual and artistic treasures of a society be too stringently restricted by personal monopolies. In a sense, the person who creates a work of art after seeing another, has contributed something of value to society. Frequently, this artist will refine prior techniques or even stimulate greater public enthusiasm for the subject matter. Most likely, this artist's creation will not materially affect the ability of the first artist to dispose of his work, and may even give the work of the first artist greater value and public acceptance.

The right or freedom to imitate does not permit an individual to copy or wrongfully appropriate the creations of another artist. The creator has every right to enjoy the economic fruits of his labors. But, as our copyright law clearly recognizes, the artist should not be entitled to gain a monopoly of a theme, a subject, or an idea.

Conclusion

The legal remedies discussed in this chapter by no means exhaust the avenues of protection available to the artist. These theories of law should be a starting point, however, for the artist to determine whether any of his vested legal rights have been violated. If redress is planned, the artist should seek the advice of a competent attorney.

Chapter 4
COPYRIGHT PROTECTIONS

An artist, writer, or painter is a social being, and art is a form of communication. The author is as much flattered by the number of people who read his book as he is at the size of his royalty check. Likewise, the painter or sculptor whose work is thought worthy of acquisition for public display may receive greater satisfaction from this accomplishment than if the work is acquired by a private collector who alone will receive his message. Some artists will even waive any payment for works of art which they may create for public institutions.

Because art is in part a public activity, a myriad of legal problems may arise. As a general rule, the artist does not wish to restrict the legitimate publicity given his talents through photographs, sketches, reproductions, and the like. Yet, the artist properly concerned with earning a livelihood from his work, must protect himself from publicity given for purposes of economic exploitation. How can the artist expose his works to the public, while reserving for himself alone, the rights pertaining to those works. This is the problem that has led to copyright laws.

History of Copyright Legislation

It had been established by the common, or judge-made, law of England that the creator of an intellectual work owned that work just as he did the chair upon which he sat. This ownership or property right, which prevented copying as well as stealing, continued as long as the creator did not expose his work to the public. What rights he had after exposure or publication were, at best, open to question until the enactment of the first copyright legislation in 1710, the Statute of Anne. That statute, upon which all subsequent copyright legislation is based, was enacted in response to pressure from the printing industry not too long after restrictions on entering the printing business had been lifted. With anyone able to open a printing establishment, there was always the temptation to pirate a competitor's best seller.

The old common law copyright continued to exist even in the presence of a statute but only until such time as publication was effected. The statutory copyright was available to the creator only after his work was published. This distinction continued in American law. We had until 1976 federal copyright legislation applicable once a work had been published, and common law rights, administered by the individual states, respecting works that are still in the possession of their creators.

In 1976, President Gerald R. Ford signed the Copyright Act of 1976, the first complete revision of United States copyright law since the Copyright Act of 1909. The 1909 Act, passed during the final days of Theodore Roosevelt's administration, was written before the technological explosion of the 20th century. It became outdated almost immediately after its enactment, and efforts at a complete revision began as early as 1924.

Revision efforts during the 1920s and 1930s were unsuccessful and were stalled entirely during the Second World War. After the war, the United States copyright community focused its attention upon the achievement of an international copyright treaty to which the United States would be a party. When the Universal Copyright Convention came into force in 1955, the effort to revise the outmoded 1909 Copyright Act began anew. It took twenty-one years of studies, draftsmanship, hearings, and debates to achieve this revision.

The 1976 Copyright Act represents a major advance for the creator. This is not to say that every provision is favorable to the creator. The new law is extremely complex, and the effects of many of its provisions are a continued subject of debate. This chapter will be an attempt to demonstrate how the copyright law works for the visual artist.

Federal Preemption of Copyright

Since the enactment of the first federal copyright law in 1790, the United States has had a unique and confusing dual system of copyright. After "creation" but prior to "publication" of a work, as the terms are used in the copyright sense, protection was a matter of state statutory or common law. Once "publication" took place, state common law protection ceased, and the only protection available was under the federal copyright statute. If the author did not comply with the federal copyright requirements at the time of "publication" the work lost all protection and passed into the public domain. To complicate matters more, certain types of works could be registered for federal copyright protection prior to publication, while such protection was not available to other types of unpublished works. The result was a confusing system of copyright protection like no other in the world.

This bifurcation of protection and the confusion that followed has been remedied by the new law, which abolished the dual system of copyright and substitutes a single unified system of federal copyright protection. Initially, it might appear that federal preemption worked to the detriment of the creator. State common law had extended protection in perpetuity, while federal protection, by constitutional mandate, is limited in duration. For many reasons, however, the federal preemption is a major improvement for the creator.

First, it is widely recognized that federal copyright offers far better protection than state common law. For example, in any infringement action the prima facie evidentiary weight granted to a federal copyright certificate shifts the burden of proof regarding the validity of the copyright and the facts contained in the certificate. The ability to press claims in federal courts which are familiar with copyright litigation, rather than in state courts which do not have equal sophistication, also works to the creator's advantage. A single, national, and uniform system of copyright frees the creator and his lawyer from concern over differences in the common law of the various states.

Furthermore, the abolition of state common law protection means that federal copyright need no longer be based on the concept of "publication." Therefore, the new law allows registration of all types of unpublished works, and all authors, not only those whose works attain sufficient commercial success to be published, may benefit fully from federal copyright protection. As we shall see, this advantage goes to visual artists and their artworks as well.

Copyright Term

Federal preemption of copyright protection may be the most important theoretical improvement in the new law, but in purely practical terms the most important advance is the extension of the copyright term for works copyrighted both before and after the effective date of the new law, January 1, 1978.

The 1909 law granted an initial copyright term of twenty-eight years. If the work was properly renewed in its twenty-eighth year, a renewal term of twenty-eight years was granted. Proper renewal, then, meant a total term of fifty-six years. The new 1976 law extends the total term to seventy-five years for works protected by federal copyright as of the new law's effective date by adding an additional nineteen years to the renewal term. So a work copyrighted before January 1, 1978 will have the same initial term of twenty-eight years but will be entitled to a longer renewal term of forty-seven years. The nineteen-year addition to the renewal term is automatic for works already in their renewal term on January 1, 1978. It is important to note, however, that works in their initial term on January 1, 1978 must still be renewed at the proper time to enjoy the extended term of the new law. Failure to renew properly will cause the work to pass into the public domain at the end of the initial term.

While the extension of term for already existing copyrights is important, the major advance in the term of copyright protection applies to works created or copyrighted on or after January 1, 1978. The basic term of copyright protection for such works is not a constant term of years but is based on the life of the author. Copyright will exist for the author or creator's life and for fifty years after his or her death.

A term based on the life of the creator is significant for three reasons. First, a life plus fifty-year provision satifies the constitutional doctrine seeking the promotion of science and art and the limited protection of creators. A fifty-six year term is too short a period in which to insure a creator and his dependents the fair economic benefits of his work, or to provide an incentive for creation and dissemination of that work given the increase in life expectancy since the 1909 Act. As a matter of fact, under the old 1909 law many creators saw their work go into the public domain during their lifetimes. In addition, too short a term harms a creator without providing any substantial benefit to the public, since the price of public domain works is rarely lower than the price charged for copyrighted works. With the growth of the communications media, the commercial life of many works has been substantially lengthened. A longer term offers copyright protection for those works whose value is not recognized until many years after their initial promotion.

Secondly, a term based on the life of the creator makes possible the elimination of the renewal requirement of the 1909 copyright law, thereby removing the substantial burden renewal placed upon creators.

Lastly, almost every country in the world has adopted a copyright term of the life of the creator plus fifty years or more. The sore point in international copyright relations caused by foreign countries giving longer copyright protection to American works than the United States gives to foreign works is cured by the 1976 law.

Finally, a new right, the right of termination relating both to term and transfers of copyright, is contained in the 1976 Copyright Act. Under the 1909 Act, creators had an opportunity to reclaim the rights in their works from assignees at the time of renewal. Creators usually assigned renewal rights with the original assignment of copyright. However, if a creator died before the initial term expired, the renewal right vested in the creator's surviving spouse and children, notwithstanding any assignment of the renewal rights by the creator continues to be in force. Thus, to some degree creators and their heirs were protected. In practice, recapture of the copyrights at the time of renewal did not often occur because assignees would obtain grants of contingent future interests in the renewal copyright from the creator's spouse and children while the creator was still living, which insured continued possession of the copyright during the renewal period.

Under the 1976 Act the possibility of recapture has of course been lost. Congress, therefore, created the right of termination under which the creator or his heirs may in certain circumstances recapture copyrights previously assigned, notwithstanding a contractual agreement. Two such termination rights were created. One allows recapture of works assigned before January 1, 1978 for the additional nineteen years added to the renewal term which would otherwise be a "windfall" period for the assignee. The other allows recapture of works assigned after January 1, 1978, generally thirty-five years after the assignment is made.

Improvement is Substantive Rights for Creators

The new law contains a significant clarification of the rights protected by copyright. The 1909 law contained a long list of exclusive rights of the copyright proprietor. That long and confusing list of exclusive rights has been simplified to five basic rights:

1. The right to reproduce the copyrighted work in copies or phonorecords;
2. The right to prepare derivative works
3. The right to distribute copies or phonorecords to the public by sale or other transfer of ownership or by rental lease or lending;
4. The right to perform the copyrighted work publicly;
5. The right to display the copyrighted work publicly.

Of special importance to both musical and visual artists, public broadcasting will now pay license fees for the use of nondramatic musical, pictorial, graphic, and sculptural works in its broadcasts. Such uses are subject to compulsory licensing, but no statutory license fee is set. Rather, voluntary agreements are encouraged, but if none can be worked out the license fees will be set by a new agency in the legislative branch, the Copyright Royalty Tribunal.

The compulsory license for public broadcasting is, again, of significant importance to visual artists whose pictorial, graphic, and sculptural works are displayed on public broadcasting's programs. It's safe to assume, as has been the case in the past, that public broadcasting will try to pay as little as possible for the creative works it uses. Authors and composers of musical compositions have long had national organizations such as PEN and ASCAP to license the nondramatic performance of their works and to protect their interests in negotiations with large industries like public broadcasting. Visual artists, however, have had no such national organization, and the compulsory license of pictorial, graphic, and sculptural works to public broadcasting should offer the impetus for establishment of such an organization.

Other improvements in the law concerning the visual arts should be noted. The 1976 copyright law expressly provides that ownership of copyright is distinct from ownership of the material object embodying the copyrighted work. Coupled with federal preemption of state common law copyright, the new law has the effect of overruling the common law doctrine that the sale of an unpublished material object, especially a work of visual art, carries with it the sale of the copyright in the work.

In addition, the law now clarifies the copyright owner's right to place a work of visual art on exhibition without fear of losing his copyright. There has been some problem with the law's definition of "publication" as applied to exhibitions of works of visual art. While the "public . . . display of a work does not of itself constitute publication . . . the offering to distribute copies . . . to a group of persons for purposes of further distribution . . . or public display, does constitute publication." It had been feared that the offering of a work for sale by an art gallery would thus constitute publication and would threaten loss of the work's copyright if proper notice is not affixed. But Congressional reports on the law expressly state that such is not the case.

Copyright Formalities

Creators, and especially visual artists, have been troubled by the copyright formalities of notice, deposit, and registration. Certainly from the creator's point of view the best copyright system would be one with no formalities whatsoever. Such copyright systems exist all over Europe reflecting a long-standing European cultural presumption in favor of authorship.

A great drawback of the 1909 Copyright Act and preceding copyright acts was the requirement of rigid adherence to copyright formalities. Improper placement or omission of the copyright notice almost always worked to deprive the copyright owner of his property. While the 1976 Copyright Act makes significant progress in easing the requirements for compliance with copyright formalities, the total elimination of copyright formalities is in the future. Not only that, but in many ways compliance with formalities becomes even more important under the new law.

Copyright Notice. The requirements concerning copyright notice are eased in two important ways. First, the technical requirements regarding the notice are relaxed. No longer must the notice appear in a specific location to be effective.

Rather, the 1976 law provides that it shall be placed "in such manner and location as to give reasonable notice of the claim of copyright." The Register of Copyrights is given the responsibility of prescribing by regulation specific methods of affixation and positions on various types of works, although the regulations will not be considered exhaustive.

This change in the law was especially significant for visual artists, who for many years have objected to the old law's notice requirement on the grounds that a copyright notice marred the work's artistic character. The revised law clearly intends that this shall no longer be the case. For example, in the case of paintings, the Register of Copyrights has said that she believes a notice affixed to the back of a painting, rather than the front, would satisfy the law's notice requirement.

Copyright notice has included the use of three elements: the word "Copyright," the abbreviation "Copr.," or the symbol "©"; the year of first publication; and the name of the copyright proprietor. The present law does not require the year date on pictorial, graphic, or sculptural works with accompanying text reproduced in greeting cards, postcards, stationery, jewelry, dolls, toys, or other useful articles. For all types of works, an abbreviation by which the copyright owner can be recognized, or a known alternative designation, may be substituted for the name of the copyright owner. Further, contributions, except advertisements, to collective works such as newspapers or periodicals need not bear separate notices of copyright in addition to the notice applicable to the work as a whole.

The second easing of the notice formality concerns an error in or omission of the notice. Under the 1909 Copyright Act, a substantial error in the copyright notice or the omission of the notice from published copies could cause the loss of copyright. The 1976 Copyright Act contains saving provisions in such cases. If the copyright owner's notice is omitted from copies of the work and corrective steps are taken within five years of publication, the work will not be lost to the public domain. In case of error in the copyright notice, the law now permits corrective registration. While innocent infringers may not be liable in cases of erroneous notice, under no circumstances will the copyright be lost.

Deposit of Copies

The deposit of one or more copies of the work is required by the 1976 Copyright Act upon publication. Registration of the work must be accompanied by deposit if no deposit has previously been made. In the past, the deposit requirements have been a hardship on those working in the fine arts. For example, when only fifty copies of a work of fine art are produced the requirement that one or two of the best copies be deposited is so obviously a great artistic and financial hardship in such circumstances the work shall be exempt from the deposit requirements.

Copyright Registration

Registration is entirely permissive under the Act. A single registration for a group of related works are now allowed. Further, the Register of Copyrights is directed to establish regulations permitting a single registration for a group of works by the same individual author, all first published as contributions to periodicals within a twelve-month period. Single renewal registration in similar circumstances is also allowed. These provisions will be of special help to visual artists such as cartoonists whose works are published in periodicals.

If registration is not made the copyright owner may not sue for copyright infringement. Even if registration is made subsequent to infringement, the copyright owner may lose the right to recover statutory damages and attorney's fees depending on the dates of infringement, publication, and registration. Thus copyright registration is of extreme importance, and the best advice to a creator is to register his work with the Copyright office as soon as possible—certainly immediately upon publication.

Remember also that transfers of copyright are not valid unless they are embodied in a written instrument, and no action for infringement by the transferee may be brought until the transfer is recorded in the Copyright Office.

International Copyright Conventions

The effect of International Copyright Conventions must be considered in determining what form of copyright notice to use.

In 1954, the United States ratified a major multilateral agreement covering the subject of international copyright. This agreement known as the Universal Copyright Convention brought the United States into a partnership which protects works of art copyrighted in member nations. Prior to the Universal Copyright Convention, reciprocal recognition of copyrights depended either on bilateral agreements between individual nations, or upon the covenants of the Berne Convention to which the United States was not a party.

The Universal Copyright Convention, of which the United States is a member, requires a contracting nation to accord the works by nationals of other countries party to the Convention the same degree of protection as it accords works of its own nationals. Compliance with the formalities of acquiring copyright in the various member states is excused if the notice prescribed by the Convention is followed. This notice consists of "©," the year, and the name of the proprietor of the copyright. In essence, therefore, all "foreign" published works covered by the Convention are protected automatically in contracting nations by publication with the prescribed notice.

The copyright owner should remember that under the United States Copyright Code, the notice of copyright may include either the word "Copyright," the abbreviation "Copr.," or the symbol "©." The use of the word or abbreviation in place of the symbol does not satisfy the requirements of the Universal Copyright Convention. Failure to use the legend prescribed by the Convention may protect the copyright in the United States but will not secure reciprocal protection in member nations.

In some instances, nations have become a party to more than one Convention. The Buenos Aires Convention, for example, represents the only other attempt the United States has taken toward international copyright protection on a multilateral basis. To date, some eighteen Western Hemisphere countries have ratified the Buenos Aires Convention which recites that the law of the member country must be followed initially to perfect a copyright. The words "Copyright Reserved," "All Rights Reserved," "Directos Reservados," or the equivalent would most likely meet the requirements of this Convention.

In order to gain an effective copyright in a foreign country the provisions of the applicable treaties must be examined. Where a nation is not a party to a multilateral treaty, it may be advisable to have the work of art published in that country so as to become eligible for local copyright protection. It is recommended that a lawyer be consulted before a work of art is published in a foreign country.

Conclusion

Visual artists have generally been reluctant to avail themselves of copyright protection for their work. Many artists feel that the copyright notice is an intrusion upon their artistic statement, a defacement of their work, and an excessive capitulation to the marketplace. Of more economic significance is that many dealers and collectors are reluctant to purchase works of art bearing a copyright notice.

The consequences of the failure to copyright artworks can be disastrous to the artist. Million of dollars were made on Robert Indiana's design of LOVE, but the artist received not one cent from commercial exploitation due to his failure to copyright the work. Robert Indiana now regularly copyrights his work.

Aside from artistic reluctance to utilize the copyright notice, copyright principles are not fundamentally applicable to the visual arts for they are based upon usage for multiples. The value of a work of art is in its singularity while the value of a book or a song is that it is created to be reproduced. Unlike most books, musicial works, motion pictures, sound recordings, dramatic, pantomime, and choreographic works, the initial value of a work of art usually inures to the master work or original, rather than in its reproductive potential. For monumental sculptures, the original is the final commercial outlet for exploiting the artistic notion. For other classes of copyrightable subject matter, the economic motivation for creating the work is eventual repetition or reproduction and not merely a single sale of a copy of the underlying work.

The visual artist has done fairly well under the Copyright Act of 1976 which for the first time at least implicitly recognizes the distinction between fine works of art and other subjects of copyright and provides an escape valve from the copyright notice. Under Section 101 of the Act, the term "copies" includes the original or master in which the work is first affixed. Thus, in the context of the copyright law, an original work of art comes under the definition of "copies." However, a sale of original or a small number of copies to the public without notice does not invalidate the copyrights of such works, and the copyright owner need not take any corrective action to validate the copyright involved.

The sale of an original graphic or sculptural work without copyright notice will not automatically divest the artist of his copyright. The duty to affix notice will arise when the work of art becomes a source for reproduction. Thus, the duty to affix notice will arise from multiple run reproductions, but not for very limited editions of "relatively small" numbers of such reproductions. Under Section 405(a)(2) the artist must register the work within five years after publication without notice. The artist must than make a "reasonable effort" to add the notice to all copies which have been distributed to the public after the omission has been discovered.

Other sections of the copyright law recognize certain problems and needs of the visual arts. For the first time in history, applied arts and works of artistic craftsmanship are given statutory recognition as the subject matter of copyright. The originality requirement could cause a problem for artists. Section 101 makes a distinction between designs that can at least conceptually be identified separately and exist independently from utilitarian aspects of the useful article in which they are embodied, and those designs which cannot. Only the former are copyrightable. Thus, an artist who took an automobile tire and placed his name on the rim of the tire with a copyright notice and the year of publication—clearly a possibility these days—would probably not be granted copyright protection.

Overall, the visual artist's needs have been recognized in the present revision of the copyright law. The Copyright Office itself is helpful in supplying information to those with specific copyright problems. The artist should not hesitate to write the office when he has a copyright problem. A reproduction of a helpful pamphlet for the artist planning to apply for copyright registration. (See Appendix G.)

Chapter 5
TAX PLANNING AND THE ARTIST

I. Income Taxes
Averaging Income—"Spreading Back"

A man who earns a steady income of $10,000 per year will pay less income tax in a five-year period than the man who earns $6,000 for four years and $26,000 in the fifth year. Yet both have earned a total of $50,000. This doesn't seem equitable, especially when the extraordinary income in the fifth year is the final payment on a project that has required five years to complete. It was this inequity that prompted averaging or spreading provision in the Internal Revenue Code. This provision allows the taxpayer to treat some of the extraordinary income as if it had been earned in equal parts over a five year period.

Artists obviously have a great stake in taking advantage of this provision given the cycles their income characterize—at least for the "average" artist.

"Spreading Forward"

An artist may well receive part of his income in royalties from sales, for example, of a copyrighted print or a reproduction, a book that the artist illustrated, or a commercial product the artist designed. Royalty receipts to the creator are also treated as oridinary income rather than as capital gains.

Royalty receipts, like commissions, tend to bunch up in a single year. Such receipts may be treated under the spreading provisions of the Internal Revenue Code, but in some situations the artist may be better of if he arranges with his publisher or licensee to have the income paid over several years rather than all in one year. Such an arrangement is called "spreading forward" or deferring income. As a general rule, established artists make agreements to actually spread their income forward while rising artists, whose incomes have been going up, are more likely to be benefited by the "spreading back" provisions of the Code.

An artist who expects to receive something like $50,000 in royalties can enter into an agreement limiting the royalty payments to $10,000 in any one year regardless of the fact that more royalties have accrued to his account. This spreading forward of income is permissible as long as the artist reports his income as it is received and not on an accrual basis. The artist must exercise great caution in entering into this type of agreement so as not to gain any control or economic benefit from royalties that have accrued but are not yet paid. If it appears that the artist has gained some control of or benefit from unpaid royalties, the IRS is likely to argue that the royalties have been received and are therefore taxable. Any rights to withdraw the accrued amount, any segregation of funds by the artist's payor, and any power to accelerate the payments must be scrupulously avoided. It is best to rely simply upon the general credit of the company paying the royalty than to demand any kind of note that might be interpreted an equivalent to the royalties due.

These two methods of spreading out income to reduce taxes must be considered carefully in each factual situation; what is advantageous for one taxpayer may not be for another. The artist with bunched income problems would be well advised to seek professional help before deciding which solution to accept.

Deduction of Expenses in General

The artist who claims deductions for expenses related to his work may also be called upon to show that recreation-seeking motives were subordinate to profit-seeking motives. The inquiry differs from that for collectors in that the artist may come within selection 162 of the Internal Revenue Code (hereafter referred to as the "Code"), which provides for the deduction of ordinary and necessary expenses incurred in pursuit of a trade or business. In the relatively small number of cases that have considered this question, the artist devoted substantially full time to his art work, but did not enjoy net income from the activity in the tax year. Instead, the artist sought to deduct expenses related to his art against either investment income or income of a spouse. The artist optimistically professed the expectation that his work would soon be discovered and that he would profit from appreciation in value. He contended that his activities constituted a trade or business, not a hobby, so that the net loss was deductible.

Occasionally, the great disparity between the income derived from the artworks and the expenses incurred over a substantial period of time has led the court to conclude that there was no reasonable expectation of profit. In one case, the taxpayer worked as an artist, studied and painted, and even had a one-man show in 1948. From 1950 to 1966 he sold $600 worth of paintings. For the three years in issue, 1964 to 1966, he deducted $861, $1,142, and $3,080, respectively, for paint, canvas, frames, studio, and other expenses. The court had little difficulty finding that he was not engaged in a trade or business. But sincerity without financial success has triumphed on at least one occasion. In another case, the taxpayer, who never sold any of his works, was allowed to deduct studio expenses. The court was impressed by his family's relative penury, indicating that he was no hobbyist but seriously engaged in his art.

Artists who have gained professional recognition,

particularly from their peers, have succeeded in establishing that their art is a trade or business. *Rood v. United States* concerned a sculptor of international reputation who had been a professor at the University of Minnesota and, for two years, president of National Artist's Equity. By the date of the trial he had completed 500 works of sculptor and he had sold approximately 25 percent of them. The partnership into which he entered with his second wife for the creation and sale of his sculpture made money in 1948, 1949, and from 1957 to 1959 but lost money in the years 1950 to 1956. The court found that the taxpayer entered into his sculpture with the expectation of profit, that the partnership was engaged in a trade or business, and that the losses for the years in issue were deductible.

A more recent case in this general area is *Churchman v. Commissioner,* decided under section 183 of the Code and its regulations, which spell out the factors to be taken into account in determining whether an activity is entered into for profit. Gloria Churchman, an artist, worked in a number of media but primarily was a painter. She taught courses at San Francisco State College, exhibited her painting and sculpture at galleries, and had several one-woman shows. She had been involved in artistic activities for twenty years but in none of those years did income from the sale of artwork exceed her art-related expenses. For the years in issue, 1970 to 1972, she only earned $250 in 1972 but none in the other two years. The taxpayer made posters and books in order to make her work more available to the public, and she also kept careful records.

Applying the criteria set out in Treasury Regulation 1.183-2, the Tax Court found a number of factors that militated against a finding of a trade or business—a history of losses, a lack of dependence on the income from artistic activities, and the presence of a significant recreational element. These were overborne, however, by still others that supported her claim that she carried on the activities in a businesslike fashion, had trained to become an artist, and had devoted substantial time to her artistic activities. The Tax Court emphasized the artist's involvement in nonrecreational aspects of her work, especially marketing. It considered the failure to realize current income less important in visual arts than other fields, because beginning artists first must attain a degree of public acclaim before their serious work will command a price sufficient to provide a profit. A long gestation period before profitability is to be expected and should not of itself undercut a finding that the activity was entered into with the expectation of ultimate profit.

Churchman and other cases suggest that full-time artists are likely to find the courts more receptive to their claims for deduction than are collectors who may also and often do seek deductions for expenses involved in their collecting activities. Professionalism in the form of peer recognition, attention to business detail, and training weigh heavily. Lack of current income can be excused—at least in some situations—on the ground that income has been subordinated to the need to build inventory or establish a reputation.

Thus, the artist seriously engaged in producing art as a livelihood may subtract expenses of producing art from any income received. But if he has any doubt on which side of the line he falls, recreational or business, he should consult an attorney.

Assuming that the artist is in business to sell his work, even if it is a side business, there are a number of expenses he can legitimately deduct in calculating his taxable income for the year. In order to report his taxable income, the artist should obtain the special schedule available with the basic income tax form.

In calculating the costs of goods sold on that schedule, the artist should include the cost of any materials that go into the finished product, the cost of expendable incidentals that do not go directly into the product (for example, stationery), the wages of hired help (but not wages paid the taxpayer by himself), and other items directly related to producing and selling the product. This last general category would include, for instance, the expenses incurred in traveling to the location where the work is to be exhibited for sale. Such travel must be for a genuine business purpose and the expenses claimed cannot include those of one's family.

A finding, however, that the artist is engaged in a trade or business is necessary but not sufficient condition for deductibility of many artists' expenses. Typically, a working artist will seek to deduct expenses related to his studio. If the studio is maintained independently of the artist's residence, this should present no added problem. But when the artist lives and works in the same place—a common arrangement—deduction of studio expenses must also leap the hurdle erected by section 280A of the Code. This section was added by the Tax Reform Act of 1976 to curb the deduction of expenses arising from vacation homes and home offices.

Section 280A imposes additional conditions on deductibility that an artist may find hard to meet. For example, the artist must use the studio either "exclusively" as his principle place of business or as a place of business used by his customers in meeting or dealing with him in the ordinary course of his trade or business. If the studio space doubles as living space, these criteria must be met. Moreover, the expenses allocable to the studio can be deducted only to the extent of gross income from the sale of artworks less deductions not dependent on trade or business or profit motive. This limitation may severely reduce the studio-related deductions of an artist who has few sales in a particular year.

On the other hand, artists who pass the trade or business test may be in a better position to qualify for deduction of education and travel expenses. Like any other taxpayer, an artist may deduct education expenses to maintain or improve skills but not to qualify the artist for a new trade or business. The amateur artist's expenses for art classes should, therefore, be nondeductible: They constitute an "inseparable aggregate of personal and capital expenditures." To someone who has crossed the trade or business threshold, however, the same classes properly will be treated as a deductible expense.

Although travel and entertainment questions have been litigated extensively, few cases had occasion to articulate what travel expenses might be deducted by a professional artist. Some illumination can be obtained from cases concerning travel for education by school teachers. The courts have struggled to determine whether a particular trip is related primarily to the teacher's business, the test of deductibility. When the trip was only remotely related to the occupation, the courts have denied a deduction. Thus, a European trip taken by a driver education instructor did not become deductible because he observed world traffic problems and made inquiries about vehicle codes and license requirements in other countries. This information, if learned, would not have aided materially in his teaching in California. An art teacher who traveled to the Caribbean, the Soviet Union, and Hawaii—but visited only one art museum—did not render his vacation deductible by bringing back inexpensive native handcrafts to show his classes.

The Tax Court, however, has allowed travel deductions to teachers where the travel more integrally related to the teacher taxpayer's subject matter. In *Marlin v. Com-*

missioner, both husband and wife taught school—he Latin and she history. As they toured France they visited abbeys, cathedrals, chateaux, museums, and other historical sites. The court found that she maintained and improved her skills as a history teacher, but that visits to ancient Roman ruins were not sufficiently connected with his skills as a teacher of Latin to render his expenses deductible.

By a parity of reasoning, the practicing artist may require travel to repositories of art. Artists traditionally have learned much from study of the old masters. A trip to Paris to visit the Louvre, to Florence to view Renaissance painting, or to New York to observe *avant garde* styles, if the primary purpose of the travel is study, it should be deductible under section 162.

Foreign Transactions

Section 911 of the Code provides an exclusion from United States taxable income for income earned abroad. The question of the correct characterization of foreign income to artists was squarely addressed in the case of *Tobey v. Commissioner.* The IRS had consistently maintained in the previous cases that the artist Tobey's income constituted gain from the sale of property (his paintings) and not sale of personal services. The Tax Court, however, rejected the distinction between a sale of services and a sale of the property rights in which the services are embodied. It concluded that the relevant concern in section 911 is to distinguish personal service income from income derived from capital. For this purpose, the court said, the artist should be viewed as a taxpayer who deals in services rather than as an entrepreneur who makes a product. The court drew support from the qualified plan provision of the Code that treats gains of an artist from the sale of his work as earned income.

The *Tobey* reasoning has been applied with equal force to the source rules under sections 861-863. The source rules determine when income is derived from sources within the United States and have numerous applications with regard to the taxation of international transactions. Under these rules, the source of gain from the sale of personal property is the place where right, title, and interest in the property passes, whereas the source of services income generally is the place where the services are performed.

The Foreign Earned Income Act of 1978 revised the treatment of income earned abroad primarily by replacing the fixed dollar exclusion under section 911 with a series of deductions reflecting cost-of-living differentials, housing expenses, and other special living conditions. But the issues passed in the *Tobey* case remain important for the American artist living abroad because the deduction may not exceed earned income from sources outside the United States.

Prizes and Awards

Artists frequently receive prizes or awards for outstanding accomplishments in their field of interest. Generally, prizes and awards are includible in the artist's gross income, except in the case of scholarship and fellowship awards, or where an award is made for religious, charitable, scientific, educational, literary, or other civic achievement. For such an award to be tax free the artist must have been selected without any action on his part, and he must not be required to render substantial future service as a condition to receiving the award. However, such an award does not become taxable merely because the artist submits a written application or makes a personal appearance to plead his case.

If an award or prize does not fall within the exceptions listed, it will be fully taxable. If the prize is other than cash, the income is measured by the fair market value of the prize on the day it is received.

Donating Art to Charity

Most sophisticated art collectors realize that under the tax laws they are entitled to claim a deduction for the fair market value of art that is donated to a recognized charity. By the same token, is the artist who creates art entitled to take a charitable dedication for donating one of his own works to a charitable institution?

It is conceded that the strength of the artist's claim to a charitable deduction for donating his own work is a confused area of the law. The problem is that a person cannot take a deduction for the value of services rendered to a charitable organization. For instance, a public relations expert cannot say: "My time is worth $100 an hour and I have spent 50 hours organizing a fund drive for my church, so I will deduct $5,000 as a charitable contribution." The position of the IRS is that a person should not be permitted to take charitable deductions for the value of time spent in making telephone calls, licking stamps, or standing on a street corner with a collection box. Such contributions of time are likely to be leisure activities, not a contribution of time taken from otherwise productive activities.

On the other hand, if a man who manufactures iron pipe, chooses to give some of that pipe to his church for use in the construction of a new building, he can deduct the difference between the market value of the pipe and the costs and expenses incurred in producing the contributed property. In essence, the issue is whether the artist painting a picture resembles the public relations man giving his time, or the manufacturer donating his product.

The courts have infrequently held that an artist may deduct the value of paintings contributed to a charitable institution. But the outcome in such cases might have been different if the artist had been asked to paint a mural. If the artist donates a painting which he has set aside originally for sale, the resemblance to the manufacturer of pipes becomes more apparent. On the other hand, when the artist paints a picture on request, he resembles the public relations man who voluntarily performed a service.

If an artist claims a deduction for the contribution of his art, he is likely to be questioned by the IRS. Therefore, in order to gain a deduction for the value of a charitable donation, it is advisable for the artist to contribute a work of art he has already created, which is part of his ordinary stock in trade, rather than to create a work of art for the sole purpose of making a charitable contribution. This is based on the supposition that an artist cannot take a charitable deduction for the value of his services, but that he can deduct as a charitable contribution the value of the finished work he contributes. Where the artist contributes one of his completed works, the value of his charitable contribution is calculated by subtracting his costs of producing the painting from its market value.

In making a contribution in kind, the valuation placed on a contribution is a likely source of disagreement between the taxpayer and the IRS. If the artist has a record of sales of comparable pieces, establishing value is relatively easy. However, even without the benefit of such records, some deduction may be allowed. Where the artist was able to produce only limited evidence of market value, one court reduced the artist's valuation considerably but nevertheless allowed a deduction. For purposes of substantiating a deduction for the donation of a work of art, it is recommended that the artist hire at least three independent appraisers. Although such evidence is by no means binding on the IRS, it will no doubt be considered in valuing the deduction.

In common with donations made by any taxpayer, an artist's charitable contributions will not be deductible where they exceed in the tax year specified percentages of his adjusted gross income for that year (the percentage depending upon the type of institution to which the contribution is made). Again, this is a matter which the artist should check out either at the IRS office in his area or with an attorney.

Foreign Artists Earning Income in the United States

Once we have sorted out resident aliens from the non-resident aliens, we can proceed to examine the tax rates applicable to each group. A resident alien is an individual present in the United States who is not a mere transient and who has no definite intention to terminate his stay. By contrast, an individual who comes to the United States for a particular purpose and can accomplish that purpose promptly, is a transient or a non-resident alien. Under current regulations, all aliens, because of their alienage, are persumed to be non-residents unless they have (1) filed a declaration of intention to become a United States citizen under the naturalization law; (2) filed a required certificate of residence; or (3) performed certain acts which reveal a definite intention to acquire residence in the United States.

A *resident* alien is generally subject to the same income

tax liabilities as a United States citizen, including liability for income earned outside the United States; however, to take advantage of the joint return privilege, both husband and wife must be residents. If a resident alien pays a tax to a foreign country he is allowed a credit for such taxes on his United States income tax return if the country of which he is a *citizen* allows a similar credit to Americans. The reciprocity is required from the country of the alien's citizenship even if this is not the country to which he paid taxes for which he is claiming the credit. If the resident alien cannot claim a credit, he can still take a deduction on his United States income tax return for any foreign taxes paid.

Non-resident aliens are classified according to whether or not they are engaged in trade or business in the United States. As a rule, if personal services are performed in the United States at any time during the year, this would qualify the individual as one being engaged in trade or business. One so engaged is taxed on income derived from sources in the United States at the same rate as United States citizens and is allowed essentially the same deductions with respect to that income. Those not engaged in trade or business in the United States are further divided into two classes, depending on whether their total income from sources within the United States is more or less than a specified amount. For the percentage involved, check with the current IRS Code and Regulations.

II. Pre-Death Estate Planning

What Makes up the Artist's Estate and How it is Taxed

The artist's estate for federal estate tax purposes is computed the same way as for other persons. It includes the value of all works as well as other assets owned by the artist at his death and is reduced by deductions allowed by the Internal Revenue Code.

The "gross estate" includes all works directly or indirectly owned by the artist who is a citizen or resident of the United States at the time of the artist's death. This will include not only works actually owned, but also:

(a) Works which have been transferred legally to another, without receiving fair consideration, in which the artist has retained for his life the right to hold or show the work himself or the right to designate either alone or in conjunction with another who shall possess or enjoy the work while the artist is alive;

(b) Works which have been transferred, without receiving fair consideration, where the possession or enjoyment is actually postponed until the artist's death, and there existed the possibility that if the transferee predeceased the artist, the work would return to the artist;

(c) Works which have been transferred, without receiving fair, consideration, subject to the artist's right to revoke or modify the terms of the transfer;

(d) Works which were transferred, without receiving fair consideration (and without the retention of any rights referred to in (a-c) within three years of the artist's death, unless the value of the work at the time of transfer did not require the filing of a gift tax return by the donor;

In addition, the U.S. citizen or resident artist's gross estate will consist of all other property, real and personal, tangible or intangible, wherever situated, including, without limitation, the proceeds of insurance on the artist's life, jointly owned property and the proceeds of certain pension or profit-sharing plans' proceeds.

Computing the Tax

The taxes assessed against an artist's estate at death are calculated by applying a rate schedule to a tax base which consists of the artist's "taxable" estate (the gross estate less deductions) plus the aggregate amount of all adjusted taxable gifts made by the artist after December 31, 1976.

Valuation

In 1965 David Smith was killed in an automobile accident. Between 1940 and 1963, his galleries had sold only 70 of his pieces yielding Smith a gross income of $100,000—an average of less than $5,000 a year. During the two years before his death, his fame increased, and his gallery sold five pieces for a total of $108,000—more than his gross earnings for the previous 23 years.

However, at his home Smith left 425 unsold pieces, all subject to death taxes. Because of Smith's growing fame and his final sales, the Internal Revenue Service valued the sculpture at $5,256,918, an amount that would have created a federal estate tax liability of $2,444,629 and additional state inheritance taxes for his heirs. The estate had cash assets of little more than $200,000. Ultimately a tax court compromised the value to $2,700,000.

The Smith case prompted painter Thomas Hart Benton to write: "The Feds have got it now so that by just comparing me with market values, they make me a multimillionaire on paper and I have got to pay taxes (on death) for which I have no money . . . the best solution would be to destroy all unsold works before I die."

In May 1976, a 67-year-old Arizona artist, Ted Degrazia, known worldwide firm his portrayals of Southwest Indians, did just that. He transported an estimated $1,500,000 of his unsold paintings into the rugged Arizona mountains and burned them in protest of laws affecting artists' estates. "My heirs couldn't afford to inherit my work."

All assets owned by an artist at his death or otherwise subject to the estate tax are to be valued at their fair market value at the date of the artist's death or six months thereafter.

In general, for tax purposes, a well-reasoned appraisal from a qualified, recognized source based upon experience in the market place of the artist's own works are accepted by the IRS and the courts in most instances. Appraisals which lack substance and have no basis in reality, on the other hand, will not be so accepted.

In the Smith case, while the artist had been critically acclaimed all of his life, success in the market place was not achieved until shortly before his death. Yet within four years after his death, substantial sales by the estate had occurred.

A partial reason for lack of sales before death may have been attributable to the fact that Smith placed an inordinately high price on the works during his lifetime so as not to cheapen or reflect lack of confidence in the works. The Tax Court in that case ultimately valued the estate by averaging the two estimates of the IRS, substracting the proposed valuation of the estate's representatives, and then multiplying the difference by 50 percent. In reaching this "Solomon-like" pronouncement, the Tax Court considered the following:

(1) The principal of "blockage"—when a large number of works must be absorbed by the market at once, the price will be something less than the fair market value of the individual items lumped together;

(2) The status of the artist's reputation at death (Smith's reputation had not fully blossomed at the time of his death);

(3) The level of acceptability of the type of works in the market place because of their size and character (Smith's works were large and nonrepresentational);

(4) The relationship of the works to all the other works (the size of works, the period of Smith's life when they were created, and their quality when compared to Smith's other works);

(5) The sales price of works sold before and after death (in considering the sales after death the Tax Court noted that sales too far removed from the date of death should not be considered, and in this case, little weight was given to sales more than two years after death; and

(6) The accessibility of the works of art (in this case, a substantial expense was involved in transporting the works to a purchaser.

Even though the Tax Court considered the above factors, it did not resolve important questions relating to the weight or importance of each. Nor did it consider all of the realities of the market place. The court's reluctance to enter into this area is perhaps evidenced by its implied acceptance of the government's appraiser's estimates, despite the fact that he had no special expertise, no knowledge of the history of the sales of Smith's works during the last year of his life, limited experience in dealing with sculpture and had never viewed the bulk of Smith's works.

What is the impact of the artist's death on the value of his works at the time of death? Once an artist has died, obviously, no more works will be produced and the public no longer must wait for a further evolution of the artist's style. Extending this argument, the value may be substantially affected by someone's ability to market this already established style. This is clearly an important factor but one which arises *after* death and should have no effect on the value of the work at death (the applicable valuation date). Valuation is apparently not to be detemined based upon subsequent events. Despite this, the subsequent events may confirm that expectations on the valuation date were reasonable and intelligent. The burden is on the artist-taxpayer to place these events in a reasonable perspective.

Does the character of the works have an effect? It is possible that the works on hand are unsold because they are less desirable works of the artist and, therefore, not worth as much as those sold before death. The individuality of each work can greatly affect value, even if only a limited number of works are available.

Is it relevant that at a certain point in the future, there may be no market for the artist's work? In the *Smith* case, the remaining works represented some of the more difficult works to dispose of. At some point, the market for many of the works may become exhausted. The court did not really question whether there were buyers in the markctplace for the 425 different pieces.

Several reforms have been proposed to remedy the situation presented by the *Smith* case. First, states could allow beneficiaries of artists' estates to defer death taxes, preferably until the art is sold. However, the approach assumes an uncertain event—the subsequent sale of the artwork.

Alternatively, states could adopt existing federal laws that permits artists' estate now to defer death taxes for five years and then pay the taxes in as many as ten annual installments at a low interest rate (4% in the federal code).

Michigan in 1980 became the first state to enact deferred payment legislation. The law allows a probate court judge to permit an artist's estate to defer inheritance tax interest-free up to 10 years.

Deferred payment allows the estate to achieve maximum value through orderly liquidation of a portion of the art each year. It recognizes that artwork lacks an inherent book value, that opportunities for sale generally are limited, and that art should be sold selectively rather than marketed immediately after the artist's death.

In 1979 Main became the first state to allow inheritance taxes to be paid with acceptable art. This law requires the state museum commission to make a determination whether art offered to pay inheritance taxes is acceptable to the state. Acceptable art must be original or noteworthy, must advance understanding of Maine's fine art traditions or of the fine arts generally, or must contribute to the state's art collection. The commission and the estate's executor must agree on valuation, and the state tax assessor must review and accept the agreement. The measure also limits the value of art so that the state may accept in any year, absent extraordinary circumstances or the willingness of the museum commission to reimburse the general fund for excess amounts. Art accepted in payment of death taxes becomes the property at the state museum.

In recent years other states and the federal government have greatly increased death tax exemptions, and several states have repealed inheritance taxes.

It may very well be that for most artists the whole question about estate taxes may be moot because of increased death tax exemptions. For example, the federal government exempts roughly $175,000 of property from taxation. If the artist is married, up to $475,000 may be exempt from the estate tax after taking into account the marital deduction and community property.

Chapter 6
THE ART COLLECTOR AND TAXES

The art collector must pay taxes on income derived from the sale of art, but, unlike the artist or the dealer who buys and sells art in the ordinary course of business, the collector may become eligible to receive preferential income tax treatment on any profit. In the hands of a collector, a work of art may be a capital asset, the sale of which will be taxed at the capital gains rate. A collector may also have tax questions should he contribute a piece of art to a charitable institution. This chapter discusses the tax consequences of a sale or a contribution of art. It also briefly deals with the inheritance tax.

If a collector who sells a work of art has owned it for the requisite holding period under the Internal Revenue Code, and is not a dealer, any gain realized from the sale should be treated as long-term capital gain, *i.e.,* it will be taxed on a more favorable basis than if it were treated as ordinary income. If the gain is treated as long-term capital gain, half of the gain can be excluded from the computation of tax completely while the other half is taxed at the applicable ordinary income tax rate.

Alternatively, the gain may be subject to a tax rate of 25 percent on the first $50,000 of such gain and a tax generally computed on one-half of the excess amount at the taxpayer's ordinary income tax rate. The alternative method of computing the taxation of the capital gain is at the election of the taxpayer. The practical effect of long-term capital gain treatment is that a maximum tax rate of 35% percent is established with respect to any such gain.

To qualify for capital gain treatment, the property which is sold or exchanged must have been owned by the taxpayer for twelve months under the Code.

If a collector buys and sells art with sufficient frequency so that the sale may be considered a "sale in the ordinary course of business to customers," the sale will not be considered to be a sale of a capital asset and any gain will be taxed at ordinary income tax rates. Also, if the art work was a gift or bequest from the artist, such work will not be considered a capital asset in the collector's hand and gain will be taxed at the ordinary (higher) rates.

A collector can attempt to avoid realization of capital gain in one tax year by selling a work for installment payments rather than one lump sum payment. To qualify for installment reporting of the sale, the payment for the work sold must be made in two or more payments, the sale price of the work must exceed $1,000, the collector cannot receive more than 30 percent of the sale price in the year of the sale, and the sale must involve a "cash" sale. If the installment method is selected, and the requirements therefor are adhered to, gain from the sale will be recognized in a pro rata manner as the payments are received by the seller.

Generally speaking, a collector will not be entitled to a deduction for loss incurred in connection with the sale of an art work. The two possibilities open to a taxpayer for claiming such a deduction are (a) to establish that he is in the trade or business of buying and selling art, or (b) to establish that he is an investor and that the art work is investment property.

Collectors will generally have difficulty in establishing that they are entitled to losses either as a result of being engaged in a trade or business or a transaction for profit.

If a collector can prove that he is an investor in art and that the art works are capital assets, he may be eligible to claim a capital loss which may be used to offset capital gain and, to a limited extent, ordinary income.

Unless a sale is an "occasional sale" or otherwise

exempt under applicable laws, the seller will be obligated to pay a sales tax under local or state law. Prior to making a sale, therefore, the collector should determine whether or not the sale will be exempt.

Section 1031 of the Code provides that no gain will be recognized and taxable if one exchanges property held for productive use in his trade or business or for investment, for other property of a like kind which will be held for such purposes.

In those cases in which a collector can establish that art works are held for an investment purpose, and just as a hobby, it would appear that section 1031 would allow a collector to avoid recognition of gain by trading one art work for another.

Should the collector be unable to substantiate the investment purpose of his ownership of the art, the collector would be taxed, at a capital gains rate (assuming the collector has owned the art for the requisite period), on the difference between fair market value of the art works received and the basis of the art work which was exchanged thereof. This would be the case with most collectors since most collect art as a hobby.

Insurance proceeds received by the collector for a destroyed or damaged work will generally be taxed at capital gains rates to the extent of the excess of such proceeds over the collector's basis in the work. A collector may defer recognition of gain resulting from insurance proceeds if he reinvests such proceeds in another art work within two years after the close of the tax year in which the insurance proceeds are received.

Charitable gifts of art works, both lifetime and testamentary (in a will), can be useful tax planning devices for a collector. Lifetime gifts can result in current deductions equal to the fair market value of the donated works which the collector may use to offset the other taxable income.

Testamentary transfers can provide estate tax deductions and may avoid the necessity of liquidating a portion of the estate in order to pay taxes on the works.

In some instances, it may even be financially beneficial to the collector to donate an art work rather than to sell it for profit, especially in cases where the collector will be paying a commission to a dealer or an auction house in connection with the sale.

Charitable gifts may take a number of different forms. In addition to the outright gift of the entire art work, other types of gifts of future interests, fractional gifts of present interest and bargain sales may offer deductible opportunities.

Subject to several important limitations, when property is contributed to a charitable organization, the amount of the charitable deduction which is allowed is the fair market value of the property at the time of the contribution. The collector who makes a charitable gift of art works and intends to deduct the value of such gifts for income tax purposes must therefore be prepared to determine and substantiate the fair market value of the gifts as of the date of transfer. Fair market value may vary with respect to the same or similar depending upon the market in which the property is sold.

It should also be borne in mind that while the regulations relating to the valuation of art works for estate tax, gift tax, and income tax (*e.g.,* charitable gift deductions) purposes are similar, they are not identical.

The burden of proving the value of a donated work is on the collector. Since it is usually quite difficult to determine the value of an art work, especially when that work is unique, an expert appraisal should be obtained for all items of greater than nominal worth.

The IRS scrutinizes charitable gifts of art very closely because of the obvious possibility of fraudulent or collusive appraisals and the possibility that the works might not be authentic. Specific requirements relating to appraisals of fine art have been promulgated by the IRS. In addition, the IRS offers a publication, "Valuation of Donated Property" which contains further information pertaining to valuation and appraisals.

If the IRS questions a valuation placed on a gift, the donor has the right, upon written request, to require the Service to furnish a written statement explaining its basis for determining a different valuation. The IRS must provide this statement within 45 days after the date of the request or the date of the Service's determination, whichever is later. If the Service has obtained an expert appraisal, the Service's response must include a copy of that appraisal.

Costs incurred by a collector in connection with the appraisal of property contributed to a charitable organization are deductible for income tax purposes.

The Code imposes significant limitations on deductions which may be taken for lifetime charitable transfers. It is important, therefore, that the collector determine before making a charitable transfer the type of organization to which the contribution is being made, the type of property which is the subject of the gift and whether the organization will be using the property for a use related to its charitable purposes.

For charitable contributions to be deductible to the donor collector, the recipient organization must qualify under the relevant section of the Code at the time of the contribution. One should check IRS publication No. 78 to establish that the prospective donee is qualified. If an organization is listed in such publication it means that it has either received a ruling or a determination letter to the effect that contributions to it will be deductible to donors as provided in the Code.

If an organization is not so listed, the prospective donar should request a copy of the organization's IRS determination letter classifying it.

The Code restricts the permissible deduction for charitable contributions of personal property to the donor's "contribution base." This is defined to mean the taxpayer's adjusted gross income computed without any regard to any net operating loss carryback for the taxable year.

Subject to the rules on related use, and the percentage limitation applicable to capital gain property, if a contribution of personal property, such as an art work, is made to the type of organization which is categorized as a public charity, the contribution is deductible up to 50 percent of the collector's contribution base. If the contribution is made to a private foundation or other non-public charity, the contribution is deductible only to the extent of 20 percent of the collector's contribution base unless the donation is made to a private foundation of the type described in the Code section 170(b)(1)(d), in which case the 50 percent limitation also applies.

If a collector should make a contribution to a public charity or other 50 percent organization in any year in excess of 50 percent of his contribution base, the excess amount may be carried forward for up to five years. Contributions to 20 percent non-public charities cannot be carried forward in this way. It is again important that before making a contribution it be determined that an organization is a "50 percent organization," or the deduction resulting from the contribution may to a great extent be lost.

If art works constitute capital gain property in the hands of the collector, and they usually will, a further limitation is imposed upon the amount deductible by the collector. Deductions for contribution of such property will be subject to a maximum deduction limitation of 30 percent of the taxpayer's contribution base. Contributions in excess of such 30 percent limitation may, however, be carried forward and deducted by the collector in the next succeeding five years.

The 30 percent limitation is not applicable to contributions of capital gain property to a 20 percent non-public charity; but the deduction for such contribution is reduced by 50 percent of any appreciation in value of the property and, after such reduction, the deduction is limited to the lesser of (a) 20 percent of the donor's contribution base, or (b) the excess of 50 percent of the donor's contribution base over the amount of charitable contributions allowable to public charities and other 50 percent organizations determined without regard to the 30 percent limitation. Unlike the case with public charities, the amount of any contribution which exceeds the percentage limitation for 20 percent non-public charities may not be carried forward to subsequent tax years.

The *related use* rule applies to charitable donations of tangible personal property made to a public charity. In addition to the percentage limitation, in the event that art works given to a public charity are not used by the donee in relation to its exempt function or purpose, the deduction will be reduced by 50 percent of the appreciated value of the property donated. This means that if the contribution is for an unrelated use, the deduction will first be reduced by 50 percent of the long-term capital gain element of value and the resulting figure will be deductible only up to 50 percent of the taxpayer's contribution base.

Thus if a work is donated to a museum for resale by it, such use may not constitute a related use. A contribution for a related use may be established by a collector in two ways—either by a showing that the property was not put to an unrelated use by the recipient organization, or by showing that at the time of contribution, it was reasonable to anticipate that the property would be put to a related use. The Regulations indicate that where an entire collection is contributed to an organization and that organization sells or otherwise disposes of an "insubstantial portion" thereof, the contribution will satisfy the related use rule.

A charitable gift, as well as a noncharitable gift, may take a number of different forms. It may be conditional, it may be a gift of only a present or future interest, it may contemplate some consideration in return thereof, or it may be a bargain sale. If the transfer is to a charitable organization the nature of the gift can have significant tax implications. The collector is advised to check with his lawyer or turn to the helpful IRS publications for further understanding of these issues.

Under our tax laws, all taxpayers are entitled to deductions for contributions made to qualifying charities. Under our tax laws there is an added advantage to a business enterprise which purchases art works as decorations and furnishings. These objects become depreciable assets—a major tax advantage. The art collector, individual as well as corporate, is in a unique position not only to gain enjoyment from his art but also to conserve taxes. Effective planning for these savings, generally requires professional advice. The collector would be short-sighted to forego legal assistance before making a charitable donation from his collection.

Chapter 7
INSURANCE MATTERS

Insurance is important to the collector, the artist, and the dealer. While money will not replace a work of art damaged or destroyed, it will at least reduce or eliminate the concomitant financial loss. For the artist, his works represent an investment of time, and undoubtedly some money. If the works are lost, so is his source of future income unless that loss is protected by insurance. For the collector, works of art may represent a considerable financial investment. If the property is lost so is a portion of the collector's personal wealth unless the collector is covered by insurance. For the dealer, his inventory may represent a substantial investment of time and money. If his stock in trade is lost, the continuity of his business may be in jeopardy unless his inventory of art is protected by insurance. Moreover, if the dealer is holding art work on consignment, he is taking the risk that he will be liable to pay the owner for property destroyed while in his possession.

Insurance as Contract

An insurance policy is a form of contract subject to the general rules of contract law. It is, however, a special type of agreement known as an "aleatory" contract. The *Concise Oxford Dictionary* defines aleatory as "depending on the throw of a die or on chance." An insurance policy is essentially a bet. The characteristic that distiguishes an aleatory from the usual bilateral contract is that one of the parties to the contract may never have to perform. Whether performance will be necessary depends solely upon the happening of an event that may never occur; the house may not burn down or the painting may not be stolen.

The laws pertaining to aleatory contracts differ in some respects from those respecting the normal bilateral contract. The tendency of the courts is to interpret the promises of each party to an aleatory contract as independent rather than dependent. If a buyer promises to pay $1,000 for the delivery of an automobile, the buyer's duty to pay is dependent upon the car being delivered. The same contrat can be drafted so that the promises are independent. For instance, the buyer promises to pay $1,000 and the seller promises to deliver a car. In that form, the buyer may have to pay regardless of whether the car is delivered, and to gain possession of the car he must go to court. The tendency of our courts, however, is to interpret non-aleatory contracts as if the promises were mutually dependent unless the independence of the promises is made absolutely clear in the agreement. In an insurance policy, however, the insurer's duty to pay upon a loss is normally held to be independent of the insured's duty to pay his premiums. If the insured misses a premium payment and then submits a claim on the policy, unless the contract provides clearly otherwise, the insurance company must pay, though the insurer may have a counterclaim for the delinquent payment.

The Formation of an Insurance Contract

Insurance is normally sold through agents, some of whom are employees of the particular company and some of whom are independent agents for a number of companies. As a general rule, the agent is not authorized to bind the insurer. Instead, the agent takes the insured's application (offer) and transmits it to the company for consideration. If the company accepts the risk, it issues a policy of insurance that becomes effective upon delivery to the insured. Should the insurer issue a policy and send it to the agent for delivery to the insured, there is some differenc of opinion whether that policy is effective and binding before the agent makes delivery to the customer.

There are times, however, when an agent is empowered to commit the insurer on a temporary basis. This may occur if the insured pays the premium upon the expectation of receiving coverage according to the terms of a specific policy. If the agent accepts the premium, the applicant will generally be insured until the company notifies him that his application has been rejected. It is advisable for the applicant to know whether the agent has the power to commit the insurer.

Subject Matter of the Insurance Contract

Most insurance of personal property is in the form of insurance protecting all the contents of a house without itemization. This would appear to be a perfectly satisfactory arrangement where no one item is of special value. But where one or more items are especially valuable, it is advisable that each article be appraised separately and scheduled in the policy. Where several items, each having considerable value, are lumped together, a problem may arise in assigning a specific value to each article. This may best be illustrated by considering the situation in which three valuable paintings are collectively insured for $50,000, and one of the paintings is destroyed. How is the value of that particular painting to be determined for insurance purposes? Or consider the situation where an auction house burns down and the house carries $1,000,000 in insurance. If the paintings in the house are owned by many different collectors, how is a value to be assigned to each painting? Problems of this nature are best avoided by scheduling each item on the master policy and reporting additional items to the insurer as they are acquired.

Types of Insurance Policies

Art may be insured under a variety of policies. For the casual collector, protection may be gained under a fire insurance policy. Generally fire insurance policies include such phrases as "household furniture," "household goods," "household effects," and "household property." Such phrases have been held to cover a variety of articles so long as the articles in question have been chiefly associated with the household in their general nature and use. Coverage has been denied where it appeared that the articles in question were not ordinarily associated with the household. By way of illustration, one court held that a Japanese vase was a part of the household furniture, and if not useful, constituted at least ornamental furniture. In purchasing a fire insurance policy, the assured is best advised to read the fine print carefully. If works of art are not included within the specified coverage, this matter should be discussed with the agent or the insurance company.

The sophisticated collector, the gallery, the dealer, or the serious artist should purchase insurance specifically designed to protect against the destruction of art. Most companies write a "Fine Arts" policy; premiums for this type of insurance are very reasonable. A "Fine Arts" policy will generally insure against risks of loss or damage to art works which are listed in a schedule attached to the master policy. However, not all risks of loss or damage are insured, and those frequently excluded are:

1. Wear and tear, gradual deterioration, moths, vermin, inherent vice or damage sustained due to and resulting from any repairing, restoration or retouching process;

2. Hostile or warlike action in time of peace or war, any weapon of war employing atomic fission or

radioactive force, insurrection or rebellion, seizure or destruction under quarantine or customs regulations, confiscation by order of any government or public authority;

3. Breakage of statuary, marbles, glassware, bric-a-brac, porcelains and similar fragile articles, unless caused by fire, lightning, aircraft, theft and/or attempted theft, tornado, windstorm, flood, earthquake, malicious damage or collision, derailment or overturn of conveyance.

Most Fine Arts policies also stipulate that in the event of total loss of any article or articles which are part of a set, the insurance company will pay the assured the full amount of the value of the set, but the assured must surrender the remaining article or articles lof the set to the company.

Most companies will offer automatic protection for a limited period of time for new acquisitions. The consideration for this coverage is generally twofold: first, the assured will pay full premium on the acquisition from the date purchased at pro rata of the policy rate; and second, the assured will report additional items of the nature usually covered by a Fine Arts policy to the company within a specified number of days after the acquisition. If a new acquisition is insured under an after-acquired clause in the policy, most companies limit liability in respect to any one loss or casualty to the actual cash value of the additional item or to a maximum of 25 percent of the total amount of the policy.

Although an insurer will normally require one or more appraisals before issuing the policy, the assured and the company may fail to agree as to the amount of loss involved. Where this occurs, most Fine Arts policies stipulate that each party may select a competent and disinterested appraiser. The appraisers must then submit their report to an umpire (either appointed by the parties or by a court of competent jurisdiction) for a decision. The decision of the umpire may be appealed to court, but in many cases the matter is settled without going to trial.

The coverage on most Fine Arts policies can be adjusted by use of endorsements. Endorsements are merely attachments which become a part of the master policy and recite the value and the amount of insurance on each scheduled item. The policy will most likely contain a clause stating that the company will not be liable for more than the amount set opposite the respective articles covered in the endorsement and that such amounts are agreed to be the values of the articles for the purpose of the policy. If a work of art appreciates in value during the effective period of the policy, it is best to so advise the company and have an amended endorsement attached to the master policy. The insurer generally includes a clause in the policy reciting that the entire policy will be void in order to avoid inflated valuations or the misrepresentation of any material fact concerning the insurance coverage.

Art Works on Exhibition or Loan

There are many instances where a person other than the owner is in possession of a work. A collector may be lending a work for exhibition, he may be selling it through an agent; an artist may be doing the same. And, of course, when in transit a work is usually in the hands of another. The liability for damage to a work in any of these situations is subject to contractual agreement—whether the owner or bailee shall be liable (see discussion on page 20), the type of insurance to be provided, and who is to pay the premium.

The person with a large collection who regularly makes parts of it available to museums and the artist who regularly ships works to galleries will probably want insurance that covers their works at all times, including while in transit and in the hands of others. Those whose pieces seldom, if ever, circulate need not bother with this extra coverage; they may arrange for it on a short term basis if the need arises.

In general, museums and galleries are likely to have blanket insurance policies covering art works they have in their possession. The difficulty of continually relisting and reappraising their exhibits is obvious, but coverage can be extended to a new work by adding endorsements to the blanket policy. The owner of the work should request certification from the insurance company that his piece has been included, by endorsement, in the master policy.

Where blanket coverage seems undesirable, the owner can and should make other arrangements. This is important because most Fine Arts policies do not cover property on the premises of any national or international exhibition unless these premises are specifically described on the policy or by endorsement. The big point with insurance is to be certain what type of coverage is wanted, which will vary from individual to individual, and to make sure that what is needed is, indeed, provided.

Loss or Destruction of Art Work

If works of art are fully insured under the provisions of an effective policy, the cost of the damage or loss will be borne by the insurance company. This does not mean, however, that the owner of an art work may insure his possession with more than one insurance company and expect to collect the full value of the lost or damaged article for each insurer. Most Fine Arts policies specify that if there is other insurance on the property at the time of loss, the insurer will be liable only in proportion to that insurer's share of all insurance on the property. In this way, insurance companies seek to protect themselves from excessive payouts.

The Internal Revenue Code provides that an individual taxpayer may deduct certain losses not compensated for by insurance or otherwise. The deduction is limited to losses incurred in a trade or business, losses incurred in any transaction entered into for profit, and any losses arising from fire, storm, shipwreck, or other casualty. If the loss involves *business* property, the difference between the value of the property immediately preceding the casualty and its value immediately thereafter may be deducted. A loss to a *personal* asset (not used for business or profit), however, is deductible only to the extent that each such loss exceeds $100. Moreover, there must be a sudden, unexpected, or unusual cause which precipitates the loss, rather than a gradual deterioration. It has been held that damages to personal assets by a flood, a bursting boiler, an act of vandalism, or a "sonic boom" are proper allowances.

In order to substantiate a loss for income tax purposes, the taxpayer must submit evidence in support of the cost or other basis of the property. In one case where the taxpayer could not prove the basis for a painting given to him, he was denied full recovery, but he had spent $100 to have the picture cleaned and prepared for sale. The Tax Court held that since the transaction was entered into for profit, the sum of $100 could be deducted as a loss.

Chapter 8

INTERNATIONAL MOVEMENT OF ART

Works of art produced in foreign countries are frequently shipped into the United States. An American museum may be assembling a Renoir exhibition including pieces owned by foreign museums and collectors. A dealer in San Francisco may have purchased a fine piece of sculpture in France with an intention to resell in this country. An American tourist may have taken a liking to a piece of ancient Egyptian art and acquired it for display in his home. Commercial goods brought from one country to another are often subjected to tariff; most countries, however, do not place such duties on works of art. Though the United State has now joined the list of countries that do not levy a tax on works of art, our history in that area is, to say the least, somewhat embarrassing.

The Tariff Act of 1897, reversing earlier policies, has levied a 20 percent tax on all art works imported into the United States. By 1908, considerable opposition to this legislation had been generated resulting in the organization of the Free Art League. This organization strove to modify the Tariff Act and gained a partial victory when duties were removed from works of art more than 20 years old, and reduced on other art to 15 percent. As expected, this compromise was not acceptable to the art world. The argument was advanced that free access to art of the world would cultivate public tastes and increase the demand for the works of American artists. In light of the growth of interest in art, there is little doubt that this was a valid argument. The tariff was attacked, also, for failure to produce the anticipated revenue. Apparently the tax did not protect the American artist from foreign competition, instead it simply discouraged the importation of art into the United States.

The efforts of those individuals advocating the repeal of tariff finally met with success in 1913. In that year the duty was removed from original art works. The real problem was not solved until 1959. The problem was what, for purposes of legislation, is art? The definition of art, written into the legislation, limited the artist to the use of traditional materials just at a time when new media were being explored. For example, is the collage (the pasting of paper and other items on canvas) a form of art? The customs law, at least, did not recognize it. The law prevented also the free entry of abstract sculpture or constructions.

Faced with problems of deciding what is art in particular cases, customs officials were bound by earlier opinions of our courts which, for certain purposes, had been asked to define art. In an 1892 case, the United States Supreme Court held that not all art was entitled to free entry, but only "free fine arts." The court defined the free fine arts as those "intended solely for ornamental purposes, and included paintings in oil and water on canvas, plaster, or other material, and original statuary or marble, stone or bronze." This definition was followed in a number of later cases.

Unfortunately the collage, the piece of abstract painting and sculpture, and the construction did not comply with the judicial definition of art. The courts reasoned that Congress never intended to incorporate all beautiful and artistic objects within the duty-free range of "works of art." Rather the courts decided that "works of art" must be suggestive of natural objects as the artist sees them—*representational* in character. This rule was first successfully contested in 1928 when Constantin Brancusi's "Bird in Flight" was imported into the United States.

The "Bird in Flight" resembled a truncated propeller cast in metal. To the artist its graceful curves interpreted the flight of a bird, but the customs officers disagreed and assessed the article as a "manufacture of metal" and levied a tax on it. The decision to tax was then appealed to the Customs Court. In reversing the decision to tax, the court felt that "under the influence of modern schools of art the opinion previously held has been modified with reference to what is necessary to constitute art within the meaning of the statute." In reaching this decision, the Customs Court listened to the testimony of leading artists, sculptors, critics, and museum officials. In effect, the court took the position that it was not a judicial responsibility to decide what is art, but rather the collector of customs should rely on the opinion of art experts. The *Brancusi* case seemed to be strong authority in favor of abandoning the representational test for determining what qualifies as a work of art.

In spite of the *Brancusi* precedent, the Customs Court in 1934 retreated from its position when faced with the problem of classifying a sculptured glass vase by the French sculpture, Henri Navarre. The court observed that the designs Navarre had molded (after the glass had partially solidified) did not represent anything found in nature. Although three art experts testified that the imported vases were works of art, the court held otherwise, reasoning that these particular vases could have been produced by an artisan as well as by an artist. The court admitted that the method of manufacture and the unique appearance of the vases would certainly appeal to the artistic taste of some people, but that the art style from which these vases derived was merely decorative, and "not such as has always been held to be the practice of the free fine arts." In reaching this decision, the court not only returned to the representational standard as the true criterion for a work of art, but also suggested that the article must not serve a utilitarian purpose.

The effect of the 1934 case was to force the Collector of Customs to make a decision concerning free entry in each individual case. The Collector recognized that a work of fine art had to be representational of something in nature but found it difficult to avoid a literal interpretation in most cases. His ultimate test was probably based on whether the particular work had a title suggesting that it was supposed to represent something found in nature. Fortunately, Congress recognized the dilemma of the Customs Collector and amended the Tariff Act in 1959 to encompass within the provisions for free entry most forms of artistic expression. These amendments removed many of the judicial procedents and antiquated laws that had previously placed a tax on culture.

Original Works

The Tariff Act amendment in 1959 modified existing provisions for importing works of the free fine arts. The new legislation contained a "catch-all" clause which empowered the Collector of Customs to admit duty-free, in addition to the types of work specifically enumerated, those objects proven to represent "some school, kind or medium of the free fine arts." Such proof may be required by the Collector of Customs from an art expert to establish the status of unprecedented works, of kinds or mediums that are not listed in the Customs' schedules.

Besides making the statute open-ended, so as not to foreclose from the free entry status the products of new forms or methods of artistic expression, the statute had also to find a means of distinguishing originals and reproductions both in the plastic and graphic fields. The statutory language of the Tariff Act does not envision the free entry of mass produced works of art. On the other hand, it is recognized that "sculpture" is often produced by casting in metal or bronze from artist's models, a method that allows for the production of many castings from one model. In order to prevent the free importation of Eiffel Tower paperweights, for example, the law limits the number of castings that may be entered duty-free to ten replicas plus the original model.

Prints and Graphic Art

Similar problems of categorization arise in the grahic field due to the advances made in techniques for making original prints. According to the Print Council of America, the general requirements for an original print to be considered a work of art are threefold; first, the artist alone must have created the master image in or upon the wood block, stone, or other material used, for the sole purpose of creating a print; second, the artist either makes or directs the production of the print from the material used; and third, the artist accepts and approves the finished print.

There are four major techniques for making original prints—relief, intaglio, lithography, and stencil. Prints made by these methods should be distinguished from mere photomechanical reproductions, which may appear to the uninformed to be original prints. It behooves the purchaser to take great precaution before acquiring a purported original print since the difference in the price commanded by an original print and a reproduction may be substantial. One way to protect a purchase is to request that the dealer state on the invoice that the print purchased is an original print. Obviously, the element of forgery may also be present in purchasing a print and, in the final analysis, the best protection is education and constant exposure to prints.

To qualify for duty-free entry into the United States, the Customs' regulations specify that an eligible work be printed by hand from plates, stones, or blocks etched, drawn or engraved with hand tools. This requirement eliminates works of art that are produced by photo-chemical or other mechanical processes. As a general rule, one useful method to distinguish an original print from a reproduction is to locate the signature of the artist and the edition number of the particular print in relation to the number representing the total edition of the series. At the present time there is no limit on the number of original prints that may be entered duty-free; the limits are such as may be set by the mechanics of the process and the realities of the market place.

If the declaration to the Customs Bureau states that a print is a reproduction, the importer and anyone charged with his knowledge would be guilty of fraud if the work was later sold as an original print. Should the purchaser wish to authenticate a print before making a purchase, he should ask to examine a copy of the Customs' declaration.

Works of Art Produced by an American Artist Residing Temporarily Abroad

If an American artist temporarily resides abroad and creates a work of art during his visit, he is certainly entitled to bring his art back into this country duty-free under the exemptions granted for original works or for original prints. Interestingly though, the revised tariff schedules include, as a separate category, works of art which are productions of American artists residing temporarily abroad. Moreover, the language of this category is broader in scope than comparable sections since the word "original" is not used in describing the works of art. It would seem, therefore, that the American artist in this circumstance may be permitted to enter duty-free more than ten castings, reproductions which are not produced completely by hand, and works that, while artistic in nature, may also have some utilitarian value. Because the apparently broad coverage of this category may be restricted in practice, it would be advisable for the artist to check with the Collector of Customs before shipping into this country, works of his that might not fall under the general heading of "free fine arts."

Antiques

The collector of antiques should remember that for purposes of gaining a duty-free classification, the date of production is the deciding factor. The tariff schedule lists different dates for different classes of objects:

1. Rugs and carpets may enter duty-free if produced prior to 1701.
2. Violins, violas, violincellos, and double basses of all sizes may enter duty free if made prior to 1801.
3. Ethnographic objects made in traditional aboriginal styles may enter duty-free if produced at least 50 years prior to their date of entry.
4. All other objects may enter duty-free if made prior to 1830.

However, if any of the foregoing duty exempted items have been repaired with a substantial amount of additional material within three years prior to the date of importation, a duty is levied upon the value of the repairs at the rate which would apply to the article itself in its repaired condition.

Obviously, other art antiquities may include works admittable duty-free under the general definition of works of art. This overlap again raises the problem of the relative coverage of the different schedules.

Stained Glass Windows and Tapestrie

Duty-free status for stained glass windows and tapestries depends upon the value and intended use of each item. To be duty-free, the glass must be valued at $15 or more per square foot, be designed and produced by or under the direction of a professional artist, and be intended for use in a place of worship. Tapestries must be valued over $20 per square foot and must be fit only for use as wall hangings.

Intended Use

In addition to tariff exemptions based on the type of work, the law allows exemptions for certain intended uses. For example, where museums and other educational institutions enter what otherwise would be dutiable exhibition material, these articles are placed in a duty-free status. In certain situations, a bond must be given by the institution for the payment of lawful duties which may accrue should any of the articles be sold, transferred, or used for a purpose contrary to the provisions of the schedule authorizing duty-free admission.

In each case, the schedule classifies each item which may be imported for a duty-free use. Thus, the importer must establish to the satisfaction of the Customs Bureau that a certain object, which normally would be subject to a tariff, is to be used for a qualifying purpose.

Export Restrictions

Before mentioning some general provisions of the United States Customs Laws, the reader should recognize that while our country encourages the entry of original art, many nations control the sale and export of their art. This is done primarily to conserve national treasures. As a result, some nations require that a license be procured prior to exportation, and some nations have even reserved the right of preemption to purchase works of art which may be exported. The collector is best advised to investigate the legal restrictions before purchasing a work of art in a foreign country.

General Customs Provisions

The Customs laws provide a general duty-free allowance which each American resident returning from abroad may claim. On and after October 1, 1965, United States residents will be allowed to bring back with them $100 in duty-free merchandise based on the fair retail value, instead of the wholesale value as provided in the previous law. This means that the shipper may include within this $100 general exemption any type of category of taxable art which has been purchased abroad

Another recent change in the Customs laws eliminates the "to follow" privilege. A resident returning to this country must bring his purchases with him at the time of entry if they are to be included in the $100 exemption. This means that a tourist, who has not used his full $100 exemption, cannot order merchandise to be sent directly to his residence and then include these items in his duty-free allowance.

Declaration for Customs

A work of art, artistic antiquity, original painting, statute or other object must be declared for examination by a Customs officer in order to gain a duty-free classification. There are standard declaration forms furnished by the Bureau of Customs, to be used for different types of objects or for objects entering under different conditions. Where a work of art is brought into the United States and a duty-free status is claimed, the importer must exhibit the invoice covering the particular article, unless the Customs examinaer is satisfied that such a statement is not necesary to a proper determination of the facts.

EPILOGUE

I hope that by the time the artist is finished reading this book he is willing to agree with me that the law is facinating, even if it concerns itself at times with human cupidity, arrogance, and doublet-dealing. But even if a tast of the law leaves bitter after-effects, it is a form of preventive medicine that the artist will find useful in keeping him out of court, assuring that he is paid, and keeping as friends those with whom he does business.

A letter written by Michelangelo in 1542, which is reproduced below, is proof enough that the legal implications of an artist's activities are not peculiar to the twentieth centry.

From Rome
(October . . . ., 1542)

To Messer Luigi del Riccio.

Messer Luigi, Dear Friend,—Messer Pier Giovani has been persistently urging me to begin the painting (in the Pauline Chapel). It may readily be seen, however, that this is impossible for the next four to six days, as the plaster is not yet sufficiently dry for me to begin operations. But there is another thing that vexes me far more than the plaster, something that prevents me from living, to say nothing of painting—I mean the delay in drawing up the ratification setting aside the contracts. I feel that I have been cheated, and as a result I am in a state of desperation. I have wrung from may heart 1,400 crowns which would have enabled me to work for seven years, during which I could have made two tombs, let alone one: and I only did so that I might obtain peace and be free to serve the Pope with my whole heart. Now I find myself deprived of the money and face to face with more troubles and anxieties than ever. I did what I did about the money because the Duke (of Urbino) agreed to it, and in order to get the ratification drawn up: now that I have paid the money I cannot obtain the ratification, so that it is easy to guess what all this means without my having to write it down. Enough; it is only what I deserve for having believed in other people for thirty years and for having placed myself freely at their service: painting, sculpture, hard work and too much faith have ruined me and everything goes from bad to worse. How much better it would have been if in my early days I had been set to make sulphur matches, for then I should not have all this anxiety! I write this to vostra Signoria because, as one who wishes me well and who knows all about the matter and therefore knows the truth, you can inform the Pope what is happening, and then he may perhaps understand that I can not live, much less paint. If I had promised to begin the work, it was in the expectation of receiving the said ratification, which ought to have been given to me a month ago. I will not support this burden any longer, nor will I submit to be abused and called a swindler daily by those who have robbed me of life and honor. Only death or the Pope can save me now from any troubles.

Your Michelagniolo Buonarroti

Reproduced from "Michelangelo,"
translated and edited by Robert W. Carden
Houghton Mifflin Company (1913).

APPENDIX A

GLOSSARY OF TERMS REPRODUCED FROM THE SOTHEBY PARKE BERNET AUCTION CATALOGUE

PRINTS

Name of artist:
Subject to the terms set forth above, each lot is guaranteed to be the work of the artist whose name appears as a heading. This heading may precede a single lot or a series of lots by the same artist.

No guarantee is made with respect to the description of the lot, however, every reasonable effort is made to provide accurate information with respect to the following.

Title:
If there is a generally accepted title for the print, that title is given at the beginning of the lot description. If the work does not have a title or the title is not known to us, a descriptive title is given n brackets.

References:
Wherever possible, standard catalogues of the artist's works are cited in parentheses following the title. This is done to facilitate identification and to indicate where the reader might seek further information with respect to any of the subjects mentioned below.

Medium:
The primary medium is identified following the title or reference. The terms used are intended as a general description and may not cover all the techniques employed by the artist.

Date:
If a date is not indicated it may sometimes be found in the cited *catologue raisonnée*.

State:
Unless otherwise indicated, the print is an impression of the only state or only published state.

Quality and Condition:
When deemed relevant and within practical limitations, an attempt is made to characterize quality and to indicate significant defects in condition. If the margins are known or believed to be full (as printed or published), this is stated.

* An asterisk at the end of a description indicates that an item has not been examined outside of the frame.

Signature:
A print is described as "signed" only if it has, in our opinion, been individually signed by the artist. Signatures of doubtful authenticity may be indicated by a question mark or by such terms as "bearing a pencil signature." No mention is made of signatures in the plate.

Edition:
Within the limits of available information, every reasonable effort is made to repre-

sent fully the relevant information as to the extent of the edition or editions of a given print. If the print described is an artist's proof or *Hors Commerce*, etc., the size of the regular edition is generally given.

Framing:

"Framed" prints are sold in the frames in which they have been received. The gallery takes responsibility neither for the appearance of frames nor for their conformity to proper standards of conservation.

Measurements:

Measurements are given height before width, in millimeters and in inches. Unless otherwise indicated, etchings and engravings are measured by the maximum dimensions of the indentation produced by the plate. Woodcuts, lithographs and serigraphs are measured by the maximum dimensions of the image.

AMERICAN PAINTINGS

WITH RESPECT TO OUR ATTRIBUTION OF AUTHORSHIP AS PER PARAGRAPH II OF THE TERMS OF GUARANTEE, THE FOLLOWING TERMS APPLY:

a. CHILDE HASSAM—The work is, in our best judgment, by the named artist. This is our highest category of authenticity in the present catalogue.

b. *RUBENS PEALE—While ascribed to the named artist, no unqualified statement as to authorship is made or intended as described in Paragraph 2 under the Terms of Guarantee.

c. ATTRIBUTED TO RUBENS PEALE—In our best judgment, on the basis of style, the work can be ascribed to the named artist, but less certainty is expressed as to authorship than in the preceding categories.

WITH RESPECT TO PARAGRAPH 5 OF THE TERMS OF GUARANTEE DEALING WITH SUPPLEMENTAL MATERIAL NOT INCLUDED IN THE TERMS OF GUARANTEE, THE FOLLOWING TERMS APPLY:

a. Signed or Inscribed—Autograph signatures and inscriptions, which, in our best judgment, are in the hand of the artist, will be transcribed in print as they appear and located in one of six areas of the canvas designated as follows:

l.l.—lower left	u.l.—upper left
l.r.—lower right	u.c.—upper center
u.r.—upper right	l.c.—lower center

b. Dated—a work which is do dated and in our best judgment was executed at that date.

c. Medium—The following terms describe the surface on which the paint, watercolor, graphite or other mediums are applied:

canvas: all weaves of both cotton and linen canvases.

paper: all artists' papers including those designed for watercolor and pastel media.

board: all semi-flexible materials partially or totally composed of wood including cardboard, artist's board, plywood and other amalgamated wood surfaces.

masonite: includes the Standard Masonite Presdwood and the Tempered Presdwood that indicates the hard wallboard which is dark brown and smooth on one side and bears the impression of wire screening on the other.

panel: inflexible hardwood surfaces generally ½—1 inches in thickness, usually prepared with a gesso ground and frequently bevelled and sized.

cradled: boards and panels which have been strengthened with a brace of hardwood ribs and crosspieces.

d. Size—given in inches to the nearest ¼ inch and in centimeters (cm.); height precedes width unless otherwise stated.

e. All pictures are framed unless otherwise noted in the catalogue.

19th CENTURY PAINTINGS

Examples of typical headings used in this catalogue

*ROSA BONHEUR (French, 1822-99)
※ 1   TWO OXCARTS

Followed, under the heading *AUTHORSHIP,* by the words *ascribed to the named artist.* The work is ascribed to the named artist by an outside expert or by our own staff and such ascription is accepted as reliable by the Galleries. While this is our highest category of authenticity in the present catalogue, and is assigned only upon exercise of our best judgement, no unqualified statement as to authorship is made or intended.

ATTRIBUTED TO ROSA BONHEUR
(French, 1822-99)
■ 2 TWO OXCARTS

In our best judgement, the work can be ascribed to the artist on the basis of style, but less certainty as to authorship is expressed than in the preceding category.

PLEASE NOTE THAT ALL STATEMENTS IN THIS CATALOGUE AS TO AUTHORSHIP, PERIOD, CULTURE, SOURCE OR ORIGIN ARE QUALIFIED STATEMENTS AND ARE MADE SUBJECT TO THE PROVISIONS OF THE CONDITIONS OF SALE AND THE TERMS OF GUARANTEE PRINTED IN THIS CATALOGUE.

> Unless otherwise stated in the description, all pictures are framed, oil on canvas and all measurements given with the height preceding the width.
>
> No reference is made in individual catalogue descriptions to condition of property offered for sale. All lots are sold "as is" in accordance with Paragraph 1 of the Conditions of Sale, and Sotheby Parke Bernet Inc. makes no representation as to the conditions of any lot sold.

OLD MASTER PAINTINGS

The following are examples of the terminology used in this catalogue. PLEASE NOTE THAT ALL STATEMENTS IN THIS CATALOGUE AS TO AUTHORSHIP, PERIOD, CULTURE, SOURCE OR ORIGIN ARE QUALIFIED STATEMENTS AND ARE MADE SUBJECT TO THE PROVISIONS OF THE CONDITIONS OF SALE AND THE "TERMS OF GUARANTEE".

a "*GIOVANNI BELLINI"—followed, under the heading "AUTHORSHIP", by the words "ascribed to the named artist".

The work is ascribed to the named artist either by an outside expert or by our own staff and such ascription is accepted as reliable by the Galleries. While this is our highest category of authenticity in the present catalogue, and is assigned only upon exercise of our best judgment, no unqualified statement as to authorship is made or intended.

b ATTRIBUTED TO GIOVANNI BELLINI

In our best judgment, the work can be ascribed to the artist on the basis of style, but less certainty as to authorship is expressed than in the preceding category.

c CIRCLE OF GIOVANNI BELLINI
   In our best judgment, a work by an unknown hand closely associated with the named artist.

d STUDIO OF GIOVANNI BELLINI
   In our best judgment, a work by an unknown hand executed in the style of the artist under his direct supervision.

e SCHOOL OF ...; FOLLOWER OF GIOVANNI BELLINI
   In our best judgment a work by a pupil or follower of the artist.

f MANNER OF GIOVANNI BELLINI
   In our best judgment a work in the style of the artist, but not by him and probably of a later period.

g AFTER GIOVANNI BELLINI
   In our best judgment a copy of a known work of the artist.

h SIGNED
   A work which has a signature which in our best judgment is a recognized signature of the artist.

i DATED
   A work which is so dated and in our best judgment was executed at that date.

CHINESE EXPORT PORCELAIN

■ 1   FINE CHINESE EXPORT COFFEE CUP AND SAUCER   *CIRCA 1770*
This title states that the cup and saucer are in excellent condition and are of Chinese porcelain made for export around the year 1770. The adjective "fine" is the only adjective used to describe the condition of a lot, and refers only to the porcelain itself, and not to the quality or desirability of the decoration.

■ 2   CHINESE EXPORT COFFEE CUP AND SAUCER   *CIRCA 1770*
This states that the cup and saucer are of Chinese Export porcelain, made around 1770.

■ 3   CHINESE EXPORT COFFEE CUP AND SAUCER   *DATED 1770*
This states that the cup and saucer are of Chinese Export porcelain and that the date of manufacture, 1770, is found somewhere on the decoration of piece.

■ 4   CHINESE EXPORT COFFEE CUP AND SAUCER   *1750-70*
This states that the cup and saucer are of Chinese Export porcelain, made sometime between 1750 and 1770.

- **5 CHINESE EXPORT COFFEE CUP AND SAUCER**

    This states that the pieces are of Chinese Export porcelain, but does not specify when they were made.

- **6 'CHINESE EXPORT' COFFEE CUP AND SAUCER**

    This states that the pieces are in Chinese Export style, but does not guarantee when they were made or that they were made in China.

- **7 CHINESE EXPORT COFFEE CUP AND A SAUCER**   *CIRCA 1770*

    This states that the coffee cup and saucer are both of Chinese Export porcelain and that they both date from around 1770, but that they are not from the same service.

WEDGWOOD

FINE WEDGWOOD BLACK BASALTES CUP AND SAUCER   *1780-98*

This states that the cup and saucer are products of the Wedgwood factory, in excellent condition, made in black basaltes, and executed between 1780 and 1798. The dating of Wedgwood is very controversial, and it should be noted that precise dating is extremely difficult and a matter of personal opinion. The marks, however, are transcribed in the catalogue as they appear on the pieces (i.e. WEDGWOOD vs. Wedgwood vs. WEDGWOOD MADE IN ENGLAND).

WEDGWOOD BLACK BASALTES CUP AND SAUCER   *1780-98*

This states the same thing as the previous description, but the condition is less than excellent.

WEDGWOOD BLACK BASALTES CUP AND A SAUCER   *1780-98*

This states that the pieces are as previously described, but that the cup and saucer may not have been 'born' together.

WEDGWOOD BLACK BASALTES CUP AND SAUCER

This description guarantees that the pieces were made at the Wedgwood factory, in black basaltes, but does not specify at what date.

BLACK BASALTES CUP AND SAUCER   *18TH CENTURY*

This simply states that the pieces are made in black basaltes, but does not guarantee their country of origin, or the factory where they were produced.

EUROPEAN PORCELAIN

Examples of typical headings used in this catalogue:

■ 1 FINE SÈVRES CUP AND SAUCER   DATED 1755

This title states: the cup and saucer are in *fine* condition; both pieces were made at the Sèvres factory, and they were made in 1755. The adjective *fine* is the only adjective used in a title to describe the condition of important lots.

■ 2 SÈVRES CUP AND SAUCER   CIRCA 1755

This states that the cup and saucer were made at the Sèvres factory around the year 1755.

■ 3 APPLE-GREEN CUP AND SAUCER   SÈVRES, CIRCA 1755

This also states that the cup and saucer were made at the Sèvres factory around 1755.

■ 4 SÈVRES CUP AND A SAUCER   CIRCA 1755

Again, this states that the cup and saucer were made at the Sèvres factory around 1755, but it also indicates that the cup and saucer may not have been "born" together.

■ 5 SÈVRES CUP AND SAUCER   1740-60

This states that the cup and saucer were made at the Sèvres factory some time between 1740 and 1760.

■ 6 'SÈVRES' CUP AND SAUCER   19TH CENTURY

This states that the cup and saucer are of Sèvres type, and although of the date specified, not necessarily made at the Sèvres factory.

■ 7 SÈVRES CUP AND SAUCER

This title without a date simply states that the pieces were made at the Sèvres factory, but does not specify when.

CHINESE WORKS OF ART

1. When a piece is in our opinion of a certain period, reign or dynasty, this attribution appears in bold type, directly below the heading of the description of the lot.

   e.g. A pottery horse in our opinion of the T'ang Dynasty is catalogued as:

POTTERY FIGURE OF A HORSE
T'ANG DYNASTY

2. No firm attribution to a period is intended by any work in a description not confirmed by an attribution in bold type below the heading of the lot.

   e.g. A pottery horse of doubtful period which may, however, date wholly or in part from the T'ang Dynasty is catalogued as:

   ### T'ANG STYLE POTTERY FIGURE OF A HORSE
   ### or
   ### POTTERY FIGURE OF A HORSE

3. Where an attribution is given in the heading for a lot and there is more than one piece in the lot, all the pieces in the lot belong in our opinion to the one period unless specifically stated to be otherwise.

4. Where no attribution is given to a piece, it is of doubtful period in our opinion or of 19th or 20th century date.

AMERICAN GLASS

STIEGEL AND STIEGEL-TYPE

Refers to tableware, bottles made by the Manheim, Pennsylvania Glassworks from 1769 to 1772. The blown production is virtually impossible to identify as having been made by Stiegel Glassworks and is, therefore, universally referred to as Stiegel-type.

KEENE, COVENTRY AND STODDARD, NEW HAMPSHIRE GLASS

The production of three separate glass factories in New Hampshire consisting of bottles, flasks and blown three mold objects in a characteristically dark-amber, olive-amber and olive-green color. Preference for clear glass caused the gradual closing of these factories between 1871 and 1873.

NEW ENGLAND GLASS COMPANY,
CAMBRIDGE, MASSACHUSETTS

In operation from 1818 to 1888, producing a variety of glassware including much free-blown lead and flint glass pieces. Cheaper manufacture in the Mid-West caused the removal of the factory to Ohio in 1888.

BOSTON AND SANDWICH GLASS COMPANY, BLOWN THREE MOLD

Glass objects made with the use of a full-sized hinged mold of two, three and four pieces. Glassware of this type was produced from 1820 through 1840 primarily in Sandwich, Massachusetts on Cape Cod.

Reference numbers listed in the text to follow are quoted from George S. and Helen McKearin, *American Glass*, 1941

Glossary derived in part from, Richard Carter Barret, *A Collection Handbook of Blown and Pressed American Glass*, Bennington, Vermont, 1971

AMERICAN FURNITURE

Examples of typical headings used in this catalogue:

1 CHIPPENDALE MAHOGANY CHEST OF DRAWERS *PHILADELPHIA, C. 1760–80*

This heading, with date included, means that the piece is, in our opinion, of the period indicated with no major alterations or restorations.

2 CHIPPENDALE MAHOGANY CHEST OF DRAWERS

This heading, without inclusion of the date, indicates that in our opinion, the piece, while basically of the period, has undergone significant restoration or alteration.

3 CHIPPENDALE STYLE MAHOGANY CHEST OF DRAWERS

The inclusion of the word "style" in the heading indicates that in our opinion the piece was made as an intentional reproduction of an earlier style.

FRENCH FURNITURE

Examples of typical headings used in this catalogue:

■ 1 LOUIS XV ORMOLU-MOUNTED MARQUETRY COMMODE
MID-18TH CENTURY
This heading, with date included, means that the piece is, in our opinion, of the period indicated with no major alterations or restorations.

■ 2 LOUIS XV ORMOLU-MOUNTED
MARQUETRY COMMODE

This heading, without inclusion of the date, indicates that in our opinion, the piece, while basically of the period, has undergone significant restoration or alteration.

■ 3 LOUIS XV STYLE ORMOLU-MOUNTED
MARQUETRY COMMODE

The inclusion of the word "style" in the heading indicates that in our opinion the piece was made as an intentional reproduction of an earlier style.

ENGLISH FURNITURE

Examples of typical headings used in this catalogue:

■ 1 GEORGE III MAHOGANY CHEST OF
DRAWERS   *THIRD QUARTER 18TH CENTURY*

This heading, with date included, means that the piece is, in our opinion, of the period indicated with no major alterations or restorations.

■ 2 GEORGE III MAHOGANY CHEST OF
DRAWERS

This heading, without inclusion of the date, indicates that in our opinion, the piece, while basically of the period, has undergone significant restoration or alteration.

■ 3 GEORGE III STYLE MAHOGANY CHEST OF
DRAWERS

The inclusion of the word "style" in the heading indicates that in our opinion the piece was made as an intentional reproduction of an earlier style.

ORIENTAL RUGS

Examples of typical headings used in this catalogue:

■ 1 ANTIQUE HERAT CARPET 17TH
CENTURY

The inclusion of the "17th Century" indicates that the rug is of the period denoted.

■ 2 ANTIQUE HERAT RUG

The use of the word "antique" indicates that in our opinion the rug is at least 100 years old.

■ 3 HERAT CARPET

If no indication of age is present in the bold type heading, the rug, in our opinion, is less than 100 years old.

APPENDIX B
ARTIST-DEALER CONTRACT// ARTISTS EQUITY ASSN. INC.

Artist's Name..........................Date....

Address...

Gallery Name..................Director's Name..

Address ....

Period of Contract, from............to..........

Terms of Exhibition:

1) Number of pieces to be shown....Itemized in attached paper.

2) Cost of shipping, crating, insurance to exhibition will be paid by
from exhibition to......will be paid by.....

3) Gallery assumes full responsibility for work lost, stolen, or damaged by any possible cause, while in the gallery possession, or in transit from the gallery, to any point of shipment.

4) Printing announcements, mailing, refreshments for opening party are to be paid by the gallery.

5) Publicity for exhibition will consist of __direct mail __newspaper __radio __TV __ other
Additional clause:

Terms of Sale:

6) Commission to gallery % to artist % on retail price, of all gallery sales, of the above artist's work

7) Commission of rental fee, to gallery %
to artist   %.

8) Conditions of payment: Outright sale, due 30 days. After that 1½% interest per month on the remaining balance.

9) Time payments of customers are divided according to percentage stated above. Not to be paid later than 15 days after check is received.

10) Gallery assumes the risk of customer's credit. All losses due to bad credit risks are to be borne by the gallery.

Additional clause:
Terms of Rental:

11) Number of pieces..........itemized in attached paper.

12) To be available for rent from......to.......

13) Individual items, rented to a particular client, may be returned to the artist at expiration date of rental.

14) Work sold during rental period is subject to the same sales condition, stated in "TERMS OF SALE". Rental fee does not constitute time payment.

15) Work is insured up to $.............

16) All reproduction rights are preserved by the artist.

17) An inventory balance is to be sent to the artist every six months from the date of this agreement, at which time the gallery shall include the names and addresses of the purchasers and renters of the artist's work.

18) The artist or his representative has the right to examine the gallery records.

19) Gallery has exclusive contract with the artist in the city of...................

20) Gallery may make arrangements with dealers in other cities ___Yes ___No

21) In such arrangements as in item #20, the gallery splits its commission with the other dealer.

22) Artist's work must be shown by gallery as long as the terms of this contract.

Signed....................... Signed...........
        Artist   Dealer

APPENDIX C
SAMPLE FORMS FOR PLANNING COLLECTORS' ESTATES

FORM 1 <u>DEED OF GIFT OF ENTIRE INTEREST</u>

        WHEREAS, ... is the owner of the following paintings:

Title	Description	Artist
1.		
2.		

and

        WHEREAS, ... is desirous of giving said painting to . . . . .University upon the terms and conditions hereinafter set forth;

        NOW, THEREFORE, the undersigned does give, grant, convey and confirm unto the . . . . University all of his right, title and interest in and to said paintings upon the condition that said paintings be made generally available by the . . . . University for inspection by the general public at such time and under such regulations and upon such conditions as the . . . . . . University may reasonably impose and be utilized by the . . . . University as a part of its program for educating its students and upon the further condition that each painting be identified as being a part of the . . . . Collection by a suitable inscription or plaque.

        IN WITNESS WHEREOF, the undersigned has hereunto set his hand and seal this . . . day of . . . . . ., 1977.

                                    _____ss.
                                       Donor

_____
   Notary Public

        The above described gift is accepted by me on behalf of the . . . . University this . . . . . day of . . . . , 1977.

                                    _____
                                        President

_____
   Notary Public

FORM 2: SPECIFIC BEQUEST OF A WORK OF ART

TENTH: I give and bequeath to the . . . . Museum in the City of . . . . and the State of . . . ., the items described below:

1. Oil painting entitled ". . . . ." by . . . . dated . . . .

2. Etc.

PROVIDED, HOWEVER, if at the time of my death the . . . . Museum is not an organization described in section 2055(a) of the Internal Revenue Code of 1954, or corresponding provisions of any subsequent Federal tax laws, I give and bequeath said items to such other organization as is described in said section 2055(a) and is designated by my Executor.

FORM 3: SPECIFIC ITEMS TO UNNAMED CHARITIES

TENTH: I give and bequeath the following described items:

1. Oil painting entitled ". . . . ." by . . . . dated . . . .

2. Etc.

to such organization or organizations as my Executors, in their sole and absolute discretion, shall select, designate and appoint. The words "organization or organizations" as hereinabove used in this Clause TENTH shall be deemed to mean and include only such organization or organizations to which a transfer is deductible for Federal estate tax purposes and is described in Section 2055(a) of the Internal Revenue Code of 1954, or corresponding provision of any subsequent Federal tax laws.

FORM 4 EXPENSES FOR TANGIBLES

TENTH: . . . . . .

I direct that all expenses of insuring, storing, transporting and otherwise caring for any property bequeathed in this [Subdivision #, Clause #] shall be paid by my Executor as an expense of administration out of my general estate until actual delivery of each article of property to the legatee at the place designated by him or her.

APPENDIX D

ART APPRAISALS

ART DEALERS ASSOCIATION OF AMERICA, INC.
575 Madison Avenue
New York, N.Y. 10022

Appraisal Procedure

The Association has prepared a set of forms, of which copies are enclosed, comprising a Letter Agreement between the donor and the Association, Conditions of Appraisal and an Information Form. If the terms are satisfactory to the donor, he signs the Letter Agreement and returns it to the Association, together with a completed Information Form and three 8 x 10 inch photographs of each work to be appraised. The Association then appoints a panel of up to three appraisers made up usually of members of the Association, but if the work requires outside expertise, non-members are appointed to the panel. Each member of the panel is familiar with the market for the artist whose work is being appraised. The appraisal made by that panel is then supplied to the donor and he is billed for each appraisal at the rates which appear in the Letter Agreement.

All members of appraisal panels serve without compensation. Fees are paid to the Association and are used by the Association, which is non-profit, to defray administrative expenses.

Under the terms of the agreement with the donor and pursuant to an understanding between the Association and the Internal Revenue Service, the Association is authorized to furnish a copy of the appraisal to the Internal Revenue Service. Although we have no assurance that the IRS will accept the Association's appraisals as final and binding, we believe that over a period of time, the Association will be recognized by the IRS as a responsible agency and that its opinions will be received with respect by the Service. All the available evidence indicates that the Association is well on its way toward that goal.

CONDITIONS OF APPRAISAL

All appraisals made by the Art Dealers Association of America, Inc. (hereinafter the "Association") are made subject to the following terms and conditions:

1. The Association only makes appraisals of works already actually donated or committed for donation to a charitable or educational institution or to a museum. It does not make appraisals for insurance purposes or purely for the information of collectors.

2. Each appraisal will be the Association's opinion of the fair market value of the work of art submitted for appraisal as of the date reported by the donor as the date of gift. If a date is listed for a proposed gift too far in the future from the date of the request, an appraisal will not be made because of the Association's inability to forecast such a market value.

3. Where the Association is unable to procure sufficient evidence of market value, the Association will either (a) state that fact and give an opinion of a work's valuation based upon reasons stated by the Association; or (b) decline to make an appraisal because of the unavailability of sufficient current market information.

4. Appraisers will be designated by the Association in its sole discretion and shall be such persons, whether members of the Association or not, as in the Association's opinion are qualified to appraise or value the work submitted. Names of appraisers will not be furnished by the Association except where necessary to substantiate the Association's appraisal in connection with an audit of the donor's tax return.

5. Ordinarily, each appraisal will be made by a panel of three persons. However, the Association reserves the right to have the appraisal made by fewer than three persons where in the opinion of the Association it seems necessary or desirable.

6. The Association reserves the right at any time and for any reason to decline to appraise a work submitted for appraisal, in which event no appraisal fee or other charge shall be payable to the Association. The Association shall not be required to state its reasons for declining to appraise. Any such refusal to appraise shall not be deemed to be any opinion of the Association, its members or their officers, directors, employees or agents, regarding the work submitted for appraisal or any person or firm who is or was in any way connected with such work.

7. The Association's appraisal is not intended nor shall it be deemed in any way to reflect upon the reputation, honesty, character or integrity of any person or firm who is or was in any way connected with the work or works appraised.

LETTER AGREEMENT

Art Dealers Association of America, Inc.
575 Madison Avenue
New York, New York   10022

Gentlemen:

I request you, the Art Dealers Association of America, Inc. (hereinafter the "Association") to appraise one or more works of art belonging to me.

This letter, together with the attached "Information for Appraisal" and the Association's "Conditions of Appraisal", a copy of which you have given me and which I have read and understood, will constitute our Agreement.

I understand that the Association only makes appraisals of works of art <u>already actually donated or committed for donation</u> to a charitable or educational institution or to a museum. I therefore represent that I have in fact already either (a) actually donated or (b) committed myself to donate to a charitable or educational institution or to a msueum each work of art to be appraised. I agree that the Association may furnish a copy of its appraisal to the donee and to the Internal Revenue Service.

I will pay to the Association a fee for each work appraised based on the appraised value thereof as follows: (PLEASE NOTE NEW RATES EFFECTIVE NOVEMBER 22, 1976):

Appraised Value	Fee
Up to $2,000	$50
$2,001 to $4,999	$100
$5,000 to $9,999	$200
$10,000 to $24,999	$350
$25,000 to $49,999	$450
$50,000 to $74,999	$600
$75,000 to $99,999	$750
$100,000 and over	On the first $250,000 thereof 1%, on the second $250,000 thereof 1/2 of 1%, on any amount in excess of $500,000 a flat $4,000, and on any amount in excess of $1,000,000 a flat $5,000.

I agree to and I do hereby release the Association, its officers, directors, employees and agents, and the Association's members and their officers, directors, employees and agents from any and all liability of any kind whatsoever in any way arising from or connected with the appraisal which I have requested.

Dated:_____

INFORMATION FOR APPRAISAL

THREE PHOTOGRAPHS (preferably 8" x 10") OF THE WORK TO BE APPRAISED MUST ACCOMPANY THIS INFORMATION FORM.

Donor's Name: _____
    Address: _____ Telephone: _____
    City: _____ State: _____

Donee's Name: _____
    Address: _____
    City: _____ State: _____

Date of gift or proposed date of gift: _____
Name of Work: _____
    Artist: _____
    From whom purchased: _____
        City: _____ State: _____
    When purchased: _____ *Purchase Price _____

Medium (Circle one or fill in)
    Painting: oil, watercolor, pastel, gouache _____
    Drawing: pencil, crayon, ink _____
    Sculpture: bronze, stone, wood _____
    Graphic: lithograph (Black/White, color), etching _____

Support (Circle one or fill in)
    canvas, paper, wood _____
Dimensions: Height _____ inches Width _____ inches
Location and description of signature, date and inscription:
    Quote how signature and/or date read:

    Face (Circle two): upper, lower, right, left, center _____
    Reverse (Describe) _____
    For Sculpture: Cast No. _____ Edition size _____
Condition of Work: _____
Former owners (dealers and collectors): _____

Exhibitions of Work: _____

References in publications (books, magazine articles, exhibition catalogues): _____

[IF SPACE IS INSUFFICIENT, PLEASE SUPPLY THE INFORMATION ON ADDITIONAL PAGE.]

* This information is required by the Internal Revenue Service regulations if the purchase was made within five years of the date of gift. Where the purchase price is supplied, it will not be disclosed to the appraisal panel.

ART
APPRAISALS AND VALUATION

I. The Cardinal Rules of Valuation

   A. "The fair market value is the price at which the property would change hands between a willing seller and a willing buyer, neither being under any compulsion to buy or sell and both having reasonable knowledge of the relevant facts." Treas. Reg. 20.2031-1(b)

   B. "All relevant facts and elements of value as of the applicable valuation date shall be considered in every case." Treas. Reg. 20.2031-1(b)

   C. The burden of proof is on the taxpayer. See Eugene P. Mathias, 50 T.C. 994 (1968), where at trial taxpayer offered no testimony in support of valuation and court noted that "the two appraisal reports are not in and of themselves probative evidence" (at p. 997); court valued painting at $500 (IRS expert's valuation) rather than $12,750 claimed. See also Charles A. Weil, 26 TCM 388, Dec. 28,420(M), TC Memo 1967-78, and Tax Court Rules of Practice No. 32

   D. "The weight given an appraisal depends upon, in addition to the completeness of the report, the appraiser's familiarity with the property, experience, background, and knowledge of the facts at the time of the contribution." (IRS Pub. 561).

   E. "The appraiser's opinion is never more important than the facts upon which it is based." (IRS Pub. 561).

   F. Valuation of works of art is always a matter of opinion, judgment, prophesy--but underlying each opinion is a bundle of facts which must be carefully gathered and assembled.

APPENDIX E

AGREEMENT OF ORIGINAL TRANSFER OF WORK OF ART

This agreement made this _____ _____ day of _____, 19____ by and between
_____(hereinafter the "Artist"), residing at
_____ and
_____(hereinafter the "Collector"), residing
at _____;

WITNESSETH:
WHEREAS the Artist has created that certain work of art;

Title: _____ Identification #: _____

Date: _____ Material: _____

Dimensions: _____ Description: _____

(hereinafter "the Work"); and
WHEREAS Artist is willing to sell the Work to Collector and Collector is willing to purchase the Work from Artist subject to mutual obligations, covenants, and conditions herein; and
WHEREAS Collector and Artist recognize that the value of the Work, unlike that of an ordinary chattel, is and will be affected by each and every other work of art the Artist has created and will hereafter create, and WHEREAS the parties expect the value of the Work to increase hereafter; and
WHEREAS Collector and Artist recognize that it is fitting and proper that Artist participate in any appreciated value which may thus be created in the Work; and
WHEREAS the parties wish the integrity and clarity of the Artist's ideas and statements in the Work to be maintained and subject in part to the will or advice of the creator of the Work.
NOW, THEREFORE, in consideration of the foregoing premises and the mutual covenants hereinafter set forth and other valuable considerations the parties hereto agree as follows:

PURCHASE AND SALE. ARTICLE ONE: The Artist hereby sells to Collector and Collector hereby purchases the Work from Artist subject to all the covenants herein set forth (for the price of _____ receipt of which is hereby acknowledged) (at the agreed valuation for the purposes of this agreement of _____).

FUTURE TRANSFERS: ARTICLE TWO. Collector covenants that in the event Collector shall hereafter sell, give, grant, barter, exchange, assign, transfer, convey or alienate the Work in any manner whatsoever or if the Work shall pass by inheritance or bequest or by operation of law, or if the Work shall be destroyed and insurance proceeds paid therefor, Collector or Collector's personal representative shall:
  (a) file a current TRANSFER AGREEMENT AND RECORD in the form and containing the information set forth and called for in the specimen hereunto annexed and made a part hereof, completed and dated and subscribed by Collector or Collector's personal representative and collector's transferee with the (Artist at the address set forth above) (Artist's agent for the purpose: _____
at: _____) within thirty days of such transfer, distribution, or payment of insurance proceeds, and shall
  (b) pay a sum equal to fifteen percent (15%) of the Appreciated Value (as hereinafter defined), if any, occasioned by such transfer or distribution or payment of insurance proceeds to (Artist at the address set forth above) (Artist's agent for the purpose: _____ at: _____
_____) within thirty days of such transfer, distribution, or payment of insurance proceeds.

PRICE/VALUE. ARTICLE THREE: The "price or value" to be entered on a TRANSFER AGREEMENT AND RECORD shall be:
  (a) the actual selling price if the Work is sold for money; or
  (b) the money value of the consideration if the Work is bartered or exchanged for a valuable consideration; or
  (c) the fair market value of the Work if it is transferred in any other manner.

APPRECIATED VALUE. ARTICLE FOUR: "Appreciated Value" of the Work for the purposes of this Agreement, shall be the increase, if any, in the value or price of the Work set forth in a current duly executed and filed TRANSFER AGREEMENT AND RECORD over the price or value set forth in the last prior duly executed and filed TRANSFER AGREEMENT AND RECORD, or, if there be no prior duly executed and filed TRANSFER AGREEMENT AND RECORD, over the price or value set forth in ARTICLE ONE herein.
  (a) In the event a current duly executed TRANSFER AGREEMENT AND RECORD is not timely filed as required by ARTICLE TWO herein, Appreciated Value shall nonetheless be computed as if such current TRANSFER AGREEMENT AND RECORD had been duly executed and filed, with a price or value set forth therein equal to the actual market value of the Work at the time of the current transfer or at the time of the discovery of such transfer.

TRANSFEREES TO RATIFY AGREEEMENT. ARTICLE FIVE: Collector hereby covenants that he will not hereafter sell, give, grant, barter, exchange, assign, transfer, convey or alienate the Work in any manner whatsoever or permit the Work to pass by inheritance or bequest or by operation of law to any person without procuring such transferee's ratification and affirmation of all the terms of this Agreement and transferee's agreement to be bound hereby and to perform and fulfill all of the Collector's covenants set forth herein, said ratification, affirmation and agreement to be evidenced by such transferee's subscription of a current duly completed and filed TRANSFER AGREEMENT AND RECORD

PROVENANCE. ARTICLE SIX: Artist hereby covenants that (Artist) (Artist's agent for the purpose as set forth in ARTICLE TWO) will maintain a file and record of each and every transfer of the Work for which a TRANSFER AGREEMENT AND RECORD has been duly filed pursuant to ARTICLE TWO herein and will at the request of the Collector or Collector's successors in interest, as that interest shall appear, furnish in writing a provenance and history of the Work based upon said records and upon Collectors' notices of proposed public exhibitions and will certify in writing said provenance and history and the authenticity of the Work to Collector and his successors in interest; and, at Collector's reasonable request to critics and scholars. Said records shall be the sole property of the Artist.

EXHIBITION. ARTICLE SEVEN: Artist and Collector mutually covenant that

(a) Collector shall give Artist written notice of Collector's intention to cause or permit the Work to be exhibited to the public advising Artist of all details of such proposed exhibition which shall have been made known to Collector by the exhibitor. Said notice shall be given for each such exhibition prior to any communication to the exhibitor or the public of Collector's intention to cause or permit the Work to be exhibited to the public. Artist shall forthwith communicate to Collector and the exhibitor any and all advice or requests that he may have regarding the proposed exhibition of the Work. Collector shall not cause or permit the Work to be exhibited to the public except upon compliance with the terms of this article.

(b) Collector shall not cause or permit any public exhibition of the Work except with the consent of the Artist to each such exhibition.

(c) Artist's failure timely to respond to Collector's timely notice shall be deemed a waiver of Artist's rights under this article, in respect to such exhibition and shall operate as a consent to such exhibition and to all details thereof of which Artist shall have been given timely notice.

ARTIST'S POSSESSION. ARTICLE EIGHT: Artist and Collector mutually covenant that Artist shall have the right, upon written notice and demand to Collector made not later than 120 days prior to the proposed shipping date therefor, to possession of the Work to the public at and by a public or non-profit institution, at no expense whatsoever to Collector. Collector shall have the right to satisfactory proof of sufficient insurance and pre-paid transportation or satisfactory proof of financial responsibility therefor. Artist shall have the right to such possession of the Work for one period not to exceed sixty (60) days every five (5) years.

NON-DESTRUCTION. ARTICLE NINE: Collector covenants that Collector will not intentionally destroy, damage, alter, modify or change the Work in any way whatsoever.

REPAIRS. ARTICLE TEN: Collector covenants that in the event of any damage to the Work Collector shall consult with Artist prior to the commencement of any repairs or restoration and if practicable Artist shall be given the opportunity to make any required repairs or restoration.

RENTS. ARTICLE ELEVEN: In the event that Collector shall become entitled to any monies as rent or other compensation for the use of the Work at public exhibition, the Collector shall pay a sum equal to one-half of said monies to (Artist) (Artist's agent as set forth in ARTICLE TWO herein) within thirty (30) days of the date when Collector shall become entitled to such monies.

REPRODUCTION. ARTICLE TWELVE: Artist hereby reserves all rights whatsoever to copy or reproduce the Work. Artist shall not unreasonably refuse permission to reproduce the Work in catalogues and the like incidental to public exhibition of the Work.

NON-ASSIGNABILITY. ARTICLE THIRTEEN: No rights created in the Artist and for the Artist's benefit by the terms of this Agreement shall be assignable by Artist during the Artist's lifetime, except that nothing herein contained shall be construed as a limitation on Artist's rights under any copyright laws to which the Work may be subject.

NOTICE. ARTICLE FOURTEEN: Artist and Collector mutually covenant that there shall be permanently affixed to the Work a NOTICE of the existence of this Agreement and that ownership, transfer, exhibition and reproduction of the Work are subject to the covenants herein, said NOTICE to be in the form of the specimen hereunto annexed and made a part of this Agreement.

(a) Because the Work is of such nature that its existence or essence is represented by documentation or because documentation is deemed by Artist to be part of the Work, the permanent affixing of said NOTICE to the documentation shall satisfy the requirements of this article.

TRANSFEREES BOUND. ARTICLE FIFTEEN: In the event the Work shall hereafter be transferred or otherwise alienated from Collector or Collector's estate in any manner whatsoever, any transferee taking the Work with notice of this Agreement shall in every respect be bound and liable to perform and fulfill each and every covenant herein as if such transferee had duly made and subscribed a properly executed TRANSFER AGREEMENT AND RECORD in accordance with ARTICLE TWO and ARTICLE FIVE herein at the time the Work was transferred to him or her.

EXPIRATION. ARTICLE SIXTEEN: This Agreement and the covenants herein shall be binding upon the parties, their heirs, legatees, executors, administrators, assigns, transferees and all other successors in interest and the Collector's covenants do attach and run with the Work and shall be binding to and until twenty-one (21) years after the deaths of Artist and Artist's surviving spouse, if any, except that the covenants set forth in ARTICLE SEVEN, ARTICLE EIGHT and ARTICLE TEN herein shall be binding only during the life of the Artist.

WAIVERS NOT CONTINUING. ARTICLE SEVENTEEN: Any waiver by either party of any provision of this Agreement or of any right hereunder, shall not be deemed a continuing waiver and shall not prevent or estop such party from thereafter enforcing such provision or right, and the failure of either party to insist in any one or more instances upon the strict performance of any of the terms or provisions of this Agreement by the other party shall not be construed as a waiver or relinquishment for the future of any such terms or provisions, but the same shall continue in full force and effect.

AMENDMENT IN WRITING. ARTICLE EIGHTEEN: This Agreement shall not be subject to amendment, modification, or termination, except in writing signed by both parties.

ATTORNEYS' FEES. ARTICLE NINETEEN: In the event that either party shall hereafter bring any action upon any default in performance or observance of any covenant herein, the party aggrieved may recover reasonable attorneys' fees in addition to whatever remedies may be available to him or her.

IN WITNESS WHEREOF, the parties have set their hands and seals to this Agreement as of the day and year first above written.

SPECIMEN · SPECIMEN · SPECIMEN

NOTICE

Ownership, Transfer, Exhibition and Reproduction of this Work of Art are subject to covenants set forth in a certain Agreement made the   day of   , 19   , by and between

(Artist)

and   ,

(Collector)

the original of which is on file with   at

SPECIMEN · SPECIMEN · SPECIMEN

TRANSFER AGREEMENT AND RECORD

To:

Know ye that _____

residing at

has this day transferred all his right, title and interest in that certain Work of art known as:

Title: Identification #:

Date: Material:

Dimensions: Description:

to _____ residing at _____ ,

transferee, at the agreed price or value of   . Transferee, hereby

expressly ratifies and affirms all the terms of that certain Agreement made by and between

                                        and

on the   day of   , 19   , and agrees to be bound thereby and to perform and fulfill all of Collector's covenants set forth in said agreement.

Done this   day of   , 19

at _____

APPENDIX F
MODEL CONSIGNMENT AGREEMENT

THIS AGREEMENT made and entered into this _____ day of _____, 197____, and by and between Artist ("Artist") and Art Gallery ("Gallery");

Witnesseth:

WHEREAS, Gallery is engaged in the business of the sale of works of art; and

WHEREAS, Artist has created, expended time and labor on, and does rightfully own and possess certain works of art, more fully described in Exhibit A hereto, and desires to sell the same;

NOW, THEREFORE, in consideration of value hereby acknowledged as received, each party agrees as follows:

1. Covenants and Promises of Gallery

Gallery hereby covenants, promises, represents, agrees and acknowledges as follows:

(a) Receipt on consignment of _____ (amount) art works, as described in Exhibit hereto:

(b) To make reasonable and bona fide efforts to sell each said art work and in any event at a price not less than that listed in Exhibit B hereto unless specifically authorized by Artist, and, to that end, to display, (within _____ weeks after receipt of said art works) _____ or more of said works and, continuously thereafter, a combination of said works in that number (or more, as may subsequently be agreed upon and set forth as Exhibit C to this Agreement) for a period of _____ weeks;

(c) To exercise all due and reasonable care in the handling, display, storage, and temporary delivery to other persons of said art works until returned to the possession of Artist;

(d) To deliver to Artist on or before the end of each month during the effectiveness of this contract, a full and complete statement of inventory and account ("Statement") in approximately the form of Exhibit _____ hereto, which shall set forth the following:

    (i) the particular art work(s) sold;

    (ii) the date of such sale(s) and amount(s) and terms thereof (whether cash, barter, exchange, credit, partial payment, or other); and

(iii) the particularly-described location of all unsold art works; and whether, if in the possession of Gallery, said unsold art works are, at the time of said report, currently displayed (and for how long displayed) or not displayed.

Gallery hereby represents that said Statements shall be accurate and complete in all respects.

(e) In the event of sale of said consigned art works, to remit to Artist within a reasonable time (or _____ days) after date of sale, together with a true copy of a bill of sale for each art work or group of art works sold, (though the name of the purchaser may be omitted) _____ percentage of the consideration actually received before California sales tax; or, if the transaction were in the nature in whole or in part of an exchange, then the fair market value equivalent thereof;

PROVIDED, that, in the case of payment at time of sale of less than the full purchase price, the above percentage of the amount actually received by Gallery shall be delivered to Artist within seven (7) days after receipt thereof, as shall in like manner the same percentage of subsequent payments to Gallery;

(f) To return to Artist within _____ days after receipt of a written demand therefor, all art works consigned under this Agreement to Gallery and remaining unsold at time of said receipt;

(g) To refrain from seeking in any way to restrain Artist in the sale of any art works other than consistently with this Agreement;

[If Paragraph 2(c) below is included, then]

[PROVIDED, that, in return for the promise of Artist as set forth in paragraph 2(d) hereof, Gallery will remit an addition _____% of the consideration received from any sale covered by this Agreement over and above that percentage provided in paragraph 1(e) hereof and such additional percentage shall be paid to Artist in the same manner and at the same time as the regular percentage provided in paragraph 1(e) hereof.]

(h) If Gallery should desire to enter any of the art works covered by this Agreement in any art show in which awards are made, to obtain the written signature of Artist on any entry form used for the purpose shall be sufficient, if in writing, and if sent by registered mail, return receipt requested, to the following addresses:

Artist:

Gallery:

IN WITNESS WHEREOF, the parties hereto have executed this Agreement on the date and year first above written.

	ARTIST: _____
Address	
	GALLERY: _____
	By _____
Address	

*Developed by the Council for Assistance to the Arts [Los Angeles].

APPENDIX G
MODEL ARTIST-COLLECTOR AGREEMENT

AGREEMENT, made this ____day of_____ 19___, between_____(hereinafter referred to as the "Artist"), residing at_____ _____, and _____ (hereinafter referred to as the "Collector") residing at _____ _____.

<u>W I T N E S S E T H</u> :

WHEREAS the Artist has created a certain work of art (hereafter referred to as the "Work") which is fully described in paragraph 1 below, and

WHEREAS the Collector desires to purchase the Work from the Artist and the Artist is willing to sell the Work to the Collector upon the terms set forth in this Agreement and not otherwise,

NOW, THEREFORE, in consideration of the mutual promises set forth in this Agreement, as well as other good and valuable consideration, the receipt of which is hereby acknowledged, the parties do hereby covenant and agree as follows:

1. <u>The Transaction</u>. The Artist hereby sells to the Collector, and the Collector here-

by purchases from the Artist, for a total price of $_____, the Work, which is described and identified as follows:

Medium:_____

Dimensions:_____

Title:_____

Date:(or approximate period of creation:
_____

Size of edition:_____

2. <u>Edition and Provenance.</u>

(a) Unless otherwise indicated in the space "Size of edition: in Paragraph 1 of this Agreement, the Work is unique. If the Work is unique, the Artist hereby covenants that he shall not produce any exact duplicate of the Work; if the Work is one of an edition, the Artist hereby covenants that the size of the edition shall not increase after the date of execution of this Agreement.

(b) Upon receipt of a written request from the Collector, the Artist shall provide the Collector with a written statement attesting to the authenticity of the Work and setting forth the size of the edition, if any, of which the Work is a part.

3. <u>Care of Work.</u>

(a) So long as the Work remains in the Collector's possession, the Collector covenants to exercise reasonable care in maintaining the Work and further covenants not intentionally to alter or destroy the Work.

(b) If the Work is damaged in any manner, the Collector shall notify the Artist of the occurence and the nature of the damage and shall afford the Artist a reasonable opportunity to conduct, or to supervise, the restoration of the Work.

(c) If the Artist does not take steps to commence the restoration of the Work within thirty (30) days after receipt of notice of damage from the Collector, the Collector shall be free to make whatever arrangements he deems appropriate for the restoration of the Work.

(d) Nothing contained in this paragraph 3 shall be construed to require that the Collector cause or permit the Work to be moved from the place where it is usually kept in order to allow the Artist to conduct, or to supervise, its restoration.

4. <u>Artist's Right to Borrow.</u>

(a) The Artist reserves the right, upon giving the Collector reasonable notice of his intention to do so, to borrow the Work from the Collector in order to include it in a public exhibition of the Artist's works. The Collector shall have the right, before permitting the Artist to borrow the Work, to demand the submission, by the Artist or by the exhibiting institution, of documents evidencing adequate insurance coverage on the Work and prepayment of shipping charges to and from the exhibiting institution.

(b) The Artist shall not be entitled to borrow the Work more than once in any twelve-month period or for any single period longer than six (6) weeks.

(c) If the Artist borrows the Work for inclusion in a public exhibition, it shall be the Artist's responsibility to ensure that the exhibiting institution identifies the Work as belonging to the Collector.

5. <u>Notices to be Supplied by Collector</u>.

(a) If the Collector moves from the address set forth at the opening of this Agreement, he shall promptly notify the Artist of his new address. The Collector shall also promptly notify the Artist of any subsequent changes of address.

(b) If the C-lector lends the Work to any museum, gallery, or other institution for purposes of exhibition or otherwise, the Collector shall promptly notify the Artist that the Work has been so lent. If the Work is to be publicly exhibited, such notice shall include the name of the exhibiting institution, the title of the exhibition, the dates of the exhibition, and the name of the curator or other person, if any, in charge of the exhibition.

6. <u>Reproduction</u>.

(a) The Collector shall be entitled to permit the reproduction of the Work in books, art magazines, and exhibition caralogues, as he shall see fit.

(b) Except as provided in subparagraph (a), the Artist hereby reserves all rights whatsoever to copy or reproduce the Work and the Collector agrees not to permit the reproduction without first securing the written consent of the Artist.

(c) Nothing contained in this Paragraph 6 shall be construed as requiring that the Collector afford access to the Work for purposes of its being photographed, copied, or reproduced.

(d) /There may be inserted here a subparagraph governing the division between Artist and Collector of any fees received for a reproduction of the Work which the Artist authorizes pursuant to 8(b)./

7. <u>Transfer of Work</u>.

(a) If the Collector, at any time after the execution of this Agreement, sells the Work, he shall pay to the Artist a sum equal to fifteen percent (15%) of the excess of the gross amount realized from the sale of the Work over the price set forth in Paragraph 1 of this Agreement.

(b) If the Collector, at any time after the execution of this Agreement, exchanges, barters, or trades the Work for another work of art, he shall pay to the Artist a sum equal to fifteen percent (15%) of the excess of the fair market value of the work of art which he receives over the price set forth in Paragraph 1 of this Agreement.

(c) The Collector may, at any time, donate the Work to a museum and, in the event of such donation, no payment shall be required to be made to the Artist. If, however, at any time after the execution of this Agreement, the Collector donates the Work to any institution other than a museum and takes a tax deduction in respect of such donation, he shall pay to the Artist a sum equal to fifteen percent (15%) of the excess if the tax deduction so taken over the price set forth in Paragraph 1 of this Agreement.

(d) If the Collector, at any time after the execution of this Agreement, gives or transfers the Work to any person in any manner other than those enumerated in subparagraphs (a) through (c) of this Paragraph 7, he shall pay to the Artist a sum equal to fifteen percent (15%) of the excess of the fair market value of the Work at the time of such transfer over the price set forth in Paragraph 1 of this Agreement.

8. <u>Duration and Effect</u>. This Agreement shall remain in full force and effect until five (5) years after the death of the Artist and shall operate to bind the parties as well as their

heirs, legatees, executors, and administrators. However, the obligations imposed upon the Collector by Paragrahps 3(b) and 4 of this Agreement shall terminate immediately upon the death of the Artist.

9. <u>Construction</u>. This Agreement shall be construed in accordance with the laws of the State of _____.

10. <u>Headings</u>. Paragraph headings have been included in this Agreement solely for purposes of convenience and such headings shall not have legal effect or in any way affect the extent or interpretation of any of the terms of this Agreement.

IN WITNESS WHEREOF the parties have signed this Agreement as of the date first above written.

_____
Artist
_____
Collector

INDEX

Agency relationships, 8
Antiques, 103
Art as investment, 12
Art works on exhibition or loan, 94
Auctions
  in general, 15-16
  duty of auctioneer, 20
  legal mechanics, 16-17
  Specific performance, 19
  Uniform Commercial Code, 21
  Warranties, 18-19

Churchman v. Commissioner, 64 et seq.
Code of ethics, 12
Collector, 12 et seq.
Commissions, 1
Copying, 14
Copyright
  Copyright Act of 1976, 50
  formalities, 53
  legislative history, 45
  registration, 55
  term, 48
Customs, 105 et seq.

Dealers, 7
Death, 5
Disparagement, 41
Donating to charity, 70

Export restrictions, 104

Foreign artists, 72
Foreign transactions, 68
Forgery, 13, 27 et seq.

Formation of insurance contract, 90

Gallery purchases, 22

Imitation in art, 43
Income taxes, 61 et seq.
Informal agreements, 9
Insurance as contract, 89
International copyright conventions, 56

Libel, 38
Loss or destruction of art work, 95

Mediation and arbitration, 11

Pre-death planning, 73 et seq.
Print forgeries, 31
Prints and graphic art, 101
Purchasing from artist, 24

Rental arrangements, 23
Rental outlets, 10
Responsibility to artist, dealers, 9

Smith David, 75 et seq.
Syndications, 26

Tariff Act amendment, 100
Types of insurance policies, 92

Unfair competition, 42
Uniform Commercial Code, forgeries, 30

Valuation, 75